SAS® 9.1.3 Management Console
User's Guide

The correct bibliographic citation for this manual is as follows: SAS Institute Inc. 2006. *SAS® 9.1.3 Management Console: User's Guide*. Cary, NC: SAS Institute Inc.

SAS® 9.1.3 Management Console: User's Guide

Contents

What's New

Overview

SAS Management Console is a Java application that provides a single point of control for managing resources that are used throughout the SAS Intelligence Platform. Instead of using a separate administrative interface for each application in your computing environment, you can use the single interface in SAS Management Console to perform the administrative tasks that are required for creating and maintaining an integrated environment across multiple platforms. SAS Management Console enables you to manage the following resources:

□ server definitions

□ library definitions

□ user definitions

□ resource access controls

□ metadata repositories

□ SAS licenses

□ job schedules

□ XML maps.

SAS Management Console works by creating and maintaining metadata definitions for each computing resource or control. These metadata definitions are stored in a repository on a SAS Metadata Server, which makes them available for use by other applications.

The 9.1.3 release of SAS Management Console provides support for the SAS Scalable Performance Data (SPD) Server, enables you to import data tables into a library, enables you to schedule flows using operating system scheduling servers, provides support for grid computing, and updates resource templates.

Details

SAS Management Console now contains the following enhancements:

□ Support is added for the SAS Scalable Performance Data Server by enabling you to define SAS SPD Server libraries, servers, and schemas. You must run the Upgrade Metadata function to add support for the SAS SPD Server.

□ You can import data tables to SAS Management Console libraries by using the Import Tables wizard. The wizard lets you register existing SAS data sets in the metadata repository.

□ Resource templates for server, library, and schema definitions have been changed. Use the Upgrade Metadata function to apply the new resource templates to your metadata server. If you are upgrading a metadata server from SAS 9.1 to SAS 9.1.3, the resource template changes in SAS 9.1.2 are applied before the SAS 9.1.3 changes are applied.

□ Flows can be scheduled using operating system scheduling services. You define an operating system scheduling server in SAS Management Console, then use the Schedule Manager plug-in to submit flows to the server. The server uses operating system commands to schedule and run the flows.

□ Support is added for a grid computing configuration. Resource templates have been added for the SAS Grid Server and the Grid Monitoring Server to enable you to create a grid computing environment. A resource template has been added for the Process Manager server, which is used to schedule jobs in a grid computing environment. The SAS Grid Manager plug-in has been added to enable you to monitor the performance of a grid and to cancel jobs.

1

Introduction to SAS Management Console

What Is SAS Management Console?

SAS Management Console is a Java application that provides a single point of control for managing resources that are used throughout the Intelligence Value Chain. Rather than using a separate administrative interface for each application in your enterprise intelligence environment, you can use SAS Management Console's single interface to perform the administrative tasks required to create and maintain an integrated environment. Although SAS Management Console runs on your desktop computer, you can use it to manage resources on all platforms supported by SAS. You can use SAS Management Console to manage

- server definitions
- library definitions
- user definitions
- resource access controls
- metadata repositories
- SAS licenses
- job schedules
- XMLMaps.

SAS Management Console manages these resources and controls by creating and maintaining metadata definitions for each resource or control. The metadata definitions you can create in SAS Management Console are stored in a repository on a SAS Metadata Server, where they are available for other applications to use. For example, you can use SAS Management Console to create a metadata definition for a SAS library that specifies information such as the libref, path, and engine type. After SAS Management Console stores the metadata definition for the library in the repository on the metadata server, any other application can access the definition to access the specified library.

Figure 1.1   SAS Management Console Overview

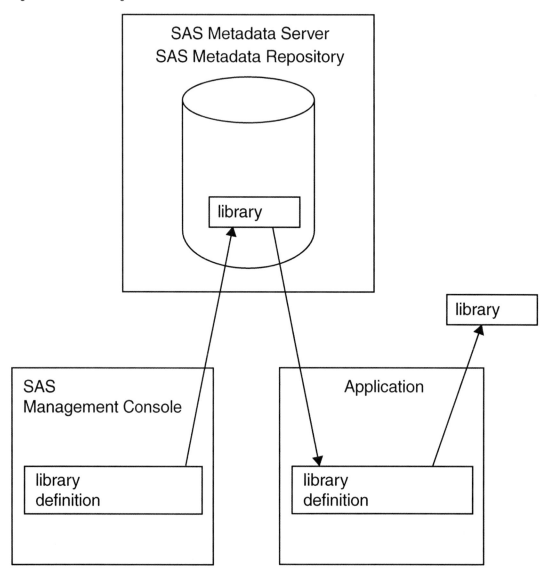

The SAS Management Console application is actually just a framework. The metadata definitions are created using plug-ins, which are application modules designed to create metadata for a specific type of resource. For example, the Server Manager plug-in creates metadata to define SAS servers and application servers. Although a set of basic plug-ins is provided with SAS Management Console, you can install other plug-ins to meet specific needs or develop your own plug-in.

How SAS Management Console Works

SAS Management Console works in conjunction with SAS Metadata Servers. You must set up and start a metadata server before you start working with SAS

Management Console. When you run SAS Management Console, you specify a metadata profile when you start the application. The metadata profile specifies the metadata server to which you will be writing metadata definitions, the active metadata repository, and information required to connect to the metadata server.

Figure 1.2 Connections to SAS Metadata Servers

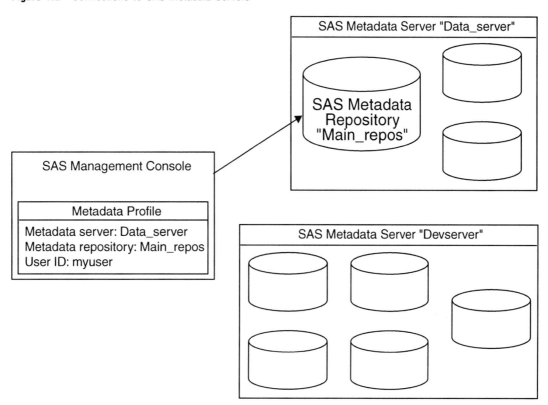

After you open the metadata profile to connect to the metadata server, you can begin using the SAS Management Console to create metadata definitions. As you create definitions, they are stored in the active repository on the metadata server. In order to use the definitions you create, other SAS applications must connect to the metadata server and repository you are using.

Each metadata server can contain multiple repositories, and you can use SAS Management Console to store definitions in any of the repositories. The repository that is currently selected and is receiving metadata definitions from the application is the active repository. You can use SAS Management Console to set up a hierarchy of repositories on the metadata server, consisting of these three repository types:

Foundation
repository
specifies the parent repository for all other repositories on the server. This repository contains resource definitions that are used throughout the server (such as user definitions).

Custom
repositories
specifies repositories that are dependent on the foundation repository or other custom repositories. A repository that is dependent on another repository accesses and uses resources from the parent.

Project
repositories
specifies dependent repositories that are intended to isolate development changes from a production environment.

You can use the three types of repositories to create a metadata environment where definitions that are widely used are stored in a foundation repository, while resources that are only needed for specialized areas are contained in custom repositories. See "Working with Metadata Repositories" on page 18 for more information about repository types.

The following figure illustrates how an organization could use each of the repository types. Global metadata (such as user definitions) is stored in the foundation repository. Each major organizational division stores division-specific metadata in the division's custom repository, and project repositories are used for making changes to the foundation and custom repositories.

Figure 1.3   Sample Repository Structure

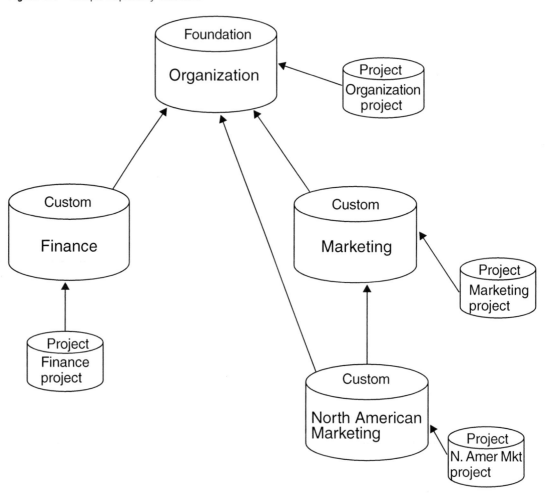

Some SAS resources, such as servers and libraries, have many different types. To make defining these resources easier, SAS Management Console uses resource templates for the definitions. A resource template is an XML file that specifies the information required to create a metadata definition for a particular resource. For example, if you wanted to define a SAS workspace server, you must first load the resource template for the SAS workspace sever. A complete set of all available resource templates is loaded automatically when you create a foundation metadata repository.

Introduction to SAS Management Console Plug-ins

When installed, SAS Management Console includes a standard set of plug-ins. Other plug-ins can be installed to access and manage other SAS or third-party applications, or can be created at your site.

The plug-ins provided with SAS Management Console are

Authorization Manager	defines access rules to control how users and groups can access metadata definitions.
Data Library Manager	creates definitions for SAS libraries and database schemas.
Metadata Manager	provides functions for defining metadata repositories on the active server, managing resource templates, and creating jobs to promote or replicate a metadata repository.
Schedule Manager	allows you to create schedules for running jobs created in SAS Data Integration Studio.
Server Manager	creates definitions for servers, including SAS application servers, database servers, and enterprise servers.
User Manager	creates definitions for users and user groups.
License Manager	allows you to view information about the SAS licenses installed on a machine, as well as details about the machine.
XMLMap Manager	allows you to import and create XMLMaps, which are XML files that describe how the SAS XML LIBNAME engine should interpret XML markup.

Working with the User Interface

The SAS Management Console user interface consists of six major parts:

1 Menu bar

2 Toolbar

3 Context bar

4 Navigation tree

5 Display area

6 Status line

Using the Navigation Tree

The navigation tree displays an organized list of all of the installed plug-ins and the objects and folders that are associated with each plug-in. The plug-ins are organized into two main categories:

Environment Management	contains plug-ins for defining metadata that applies to the overall SAS environment (such as servers, libraries, and metadata repositories).
Application Management	contains plug-ins for defining metadata that applies to specific applications, such as third-party or custom-designed applications.

Selecting a plug-in icon in the navigation tree activates the plug-in and displays folders or metadata definitions for that plug-in in the display area. To display the objects associated with the plug-in in the navigation tree, click the plus sign next to the plug-in icon to expand its contents (not all plug-ins are expandable). When you expand a plug-in, the navigation tree displays metadata definitions created by the plug-in or folders that contain sub-categories of definitions.

Using the Display Area

The display area is used to display detailed information about objects selected in the navigation tree. The information displayed depends not only on the object selected in the navigation tree, but also on the plug-in that is active. Some plug-ins (such as the User Manager) use the display area for entering information about metadata definitions.

If you select an object (plug-in or other object) in the navigation tree that contains sub-folders, the display area lists the folders.

If you select a folder in the navigation tree, the display area lists the objects that are contained in the folder.

If you select an object in the navigation tree that does not contain any sub-folders, the display area displays any metadata definitions that are associated with that object. For example, if you select a server definition in the navigation tree, the display area lists all of the connections that have been defined for the server.

Using the Context Bar

The context bar identifies the active repository, which is the metadata repository to which you are storing metadata definitions. You can select the repository that you want to access from the **Repository** drop-down list.

Using the Status Line

The status line, at the bottom of the SAS Management Console window, displays the following information:

number of objects selected	displays the number of objects selected or the number of objects contained in the currently selected folder or plug-in.
current login for the metadata profile	specifies the domain and user ID defined in the metadata profile used to log on to the active metadata server.
machine and port	specifies the machine and port number of the active metadata server.

Using the Menu Bar

The menu bar provides six standard menus and one that is controlled by the selected plug-in:

File	provides selections for opening objects, changing or closing the current metadata profile, and viewing properties for an object.
Edit	provides selections for copying, pasting, and deleting.
View	provides selections for refreshing the information displayed in the application and for moving up a level in the navigation tree.

Actions   provides selections that are valid only for the current plug-in. If no plug-in is selected, the **Actions** menu is not present. The **Actions** menu items are different for each plug-in.

Tools   provides access to an experimental metadata utility.

                        CAUTION:
                        Only experienced administrators should use this utility. Metadata errors could occur if this utility is used incorrectly. △

Roadmaps   provides access to roadmaps, which are user assistance documents designed to guide you through SAS Management Console tasks.

Help   provides options for selecting help for SAS Management Console or for the current plug-in. Help for a specific plug-in is only available when the plug-in is selected in the navigation tree.

Using the Toolbar

The toolbar provides a set of five standard tools for

☐ moving up one level in the navigation tree

☐ opening the selected object

☐ copying

☐ pasting

☐ deleting.

In addition, plug-ins can also add tools to the toolbar. The tools that are specific to a plug-in are only available when the plug-in is selected in the navigation tree. The plug-in can also provide different tools depending on the object that is selected under the plug-in. Refer to the Help or the chapters on each of the plug-ins for more information about plug–in tools.

Using User Assistance

SAS Management Console provides online user assistance through product Help and roadmaps. You can access help by selecting the **Help** menu or the ⎡Help⎤ button in SAS Management Console windows.

The help that is available from the **Help** menu depends on the plug-in that is active. If a plug-in is selected, the **Help** menu contains selections for SAS Management Console Help as well as Help for the currently active plug-in. Help for a plug-in is only available when the plug-in is selected.

Roadmaps are guides that provide the steps and brief explanations to lead you through tasks in SAS Management Console. The roadmaps are stored as XML files in the **/roadmaps** directory of your SAS Management Console installation. A default roadmap is provided with SAS Management Console, but new roadmaps to explain specific tasks can be created and installed by SAS or your organization.

CHAPTER

2

Setting up SAS Management Console

Setting Up a SAS Metadata Server

The metadata definitions that SAS Management Console creates are stored in a metadata repository on a SAS Metadata Server so that other applications and users can access them. Because of this, the first step in setting up SAS Management Console must be to define and start a metadata server. The information here is only a basic description of the process of setting up a metadata server. For detailed instructions about setting up a metadata server, see *SAS Intelligence Platform: Installation Guide*.

To set up a metadata server:

1 Determine which machine will host the metadata server. The machine must have SAS 9 or later and SAS Integration Technologies installed.

2 Create directories for the SAS Metadata Server, the repository manager, and a repository:

    a First create the server directory.

    b After you create a directory for the server, create a directory for the repository manager. This directory must be named **rposmgr** and must be located within the server directory.

    c Create a directory for the repository. Although this directory can be in any location, you may want to create it within the server directory to simplify the process of setting permissions.

3 Set access permissions to the server and server directories. Only the server invoker and user responsible for backing up the server should have access to the server directories. Some platforms require the server invoker and server accessors to have special user rights. See *SAS Intelligence Platform: Installation Guide* for information about the specific server permissions.

4 Start the metadata server. In the server directory, create a file called **startsrv.bat** with the following contents:

```
''SAS_installed_directory\sas.exe'' -nosplash -noterminal
-objectserver -objectserverparms ''protocol=bridge port=XXXX instantiate
classfactory=2887E7D7-4780-11D4--879F--00C04F38F0DB''
```

Replace *SAS_installed_directory* with the directory where SAS is installed on the server machine. Replace *XXXX* with an unused port number from 0 to 64,000. You will need the port number when you create a metadata profile in SAS Management Console to connect to this server.

Run the startsrv.bat file to start the SAS Metadata Server.

Starting SAS Management Console

On Windows, you can start SAS Management Console by selecting **Start ▶ Programs ▶ SAS ▶ SAS Management Console**You can also start the application from a command line. Navigate to the SAS Management Console installation directory and issue the command for your platform, as listed in the following table.

Table 2.1 SAS Management Console Startup Commands

Platform	Command
Windows	sasmc.exe
64-bit enabled Solaris	./sasmc
64-bit enabled AIX	./sasmc

If you do not specify any options, SAS Management Console uses the parameters specified in the sasmc.ini file. The following sections contain information about options you can specify on the command line or add to the sasmc.ini file.

Specifying Java Options

To specify Java options when you start SAS Management Console, use the **--javaopts** option and enclose the java options in single quotation marks. For example, the following command starts SAS Management Console on Windows and contains Java options that specify the locale as Japanese.

```
sasmc -javaopts '-Duser.language=ja --Duser.country=JP'
```

Specifying the Plug-In Location

By default, SAS Management Console looks for plug-ins in a **plugins** directory under the directory in which the application was installed. If you are starting SAS Management Console from another location, you must specify the location of the plug-in directory by using the **--pluginsDir** option. The syntax of the option is

```
sasmc -pluginsdir <plugin path>
```

Specifying the Error Log Location

SAS Management Console writes error information to a file named errorlog.txt in the working directory. Because each SAS Management Console session overwrites this log, you might want to specify a different name or location for the log file. Use the following option to change the error logging location.

```
sasmc -logfile ''<filepath/filename>''
```

where *filepath* is a relative path from the SAS Management Console user directory.

Specifying Message Logging

You can specify the status messages that are displayed in a SAS Management Console session by using the **--MessageLevel** *level_value* option. Valid values for *level_value* are

ALL	all messages are logged.
CONFIG	static configuration messages are logged.
FINE	basic tracing information is logged.
FINER	more detailed tracing information is logged.
FINEST	highly detailed tracing information is logged. Specify this option to debug problems with SAS server connections.
INFO	informational messages are logged.
OFF	no messages are logged.
SEVERE	messages indicating a severe failure are logged.
WARNING	messages indicating a potential problem are logged.

Creating a Metadata Profile

After you define and start a metadata server, you can start SAS Management Console. When the application starts for the first time, you must create a metadata profile. A metadata profile defines the connection between SAS Management Console and a metadata server. SAS Management Console uses the metadata profile to determine where to store the metadata definitions created in the application. You can create more than one metadata a profile to connect to different metadata servers or repositories, although only one profile can be active at a time.

To create a metadata profile:

1 Start SAS Management Console.

The Open a Metadata Profile window appears automatically if you are starting SAS Management Console for the first time.

Display 2.1   Open a Metadata Profile Window

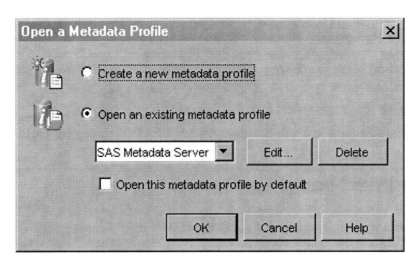

If you have already created a metadata profile, you can display this window by selecting **File ▶ Change Metadata Profile**

2 Select `Create a new metadata profile` and click $\boxed{\text{OK}}$.

3 The Metadata Profile Wizard starts. The first window explains the function of the wizard. Click $\boxed{\text{Next}}$ to continue.

4 In the Metadata Profile window, specify a name for the profile and indicate whether SAS Management Console should use the profile automatically each time the application starts.

Display 2.2   Metadata Profile Wizard – Name Window

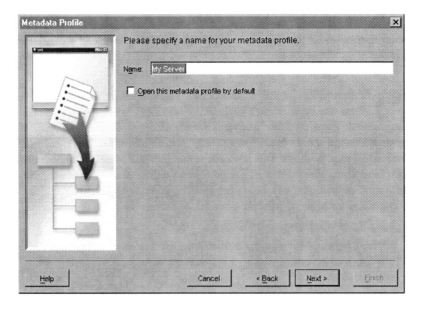

Click $\boxed{\text{Next}}$ to continue.

5 In the Connection Information window, specify the information required to connect to the machine on which the server runs.

Display 2.3 Metadata Profile Wizard – Connection Information Window

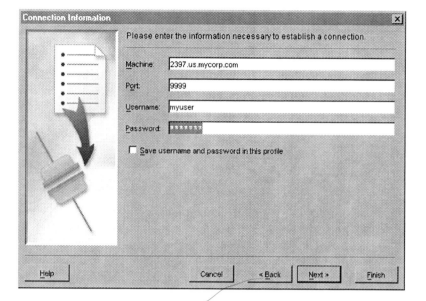

Specify the machine name and the port to connect to the server, and the user name and password to identify the credentials that will be used to connect to the machine. The port you specify must be the same port number you specified in the startsrv.bat file used to start the metadata server (see "Setting Up a SAS Metadata Server" on page 9). The user ID you specify must be one that you granted access permissions when you created the metadata server.

Specify whether the user ID and password should be stored with the metadata profile. If this option is not selected, SAS Management Console will prompt for a user ID and password each time the metadata profile is started. By not storing the logon information with the metadata profile, you can control access to the repository to only users with access rights to the repository directory. Click Next to continue.

6 The Repository Selection window lets you choose a default repository for the metadata profile. The repository you choose will be the active repository when you connect using the profile, although you can switch to a different repository after you are connected to the server.

Display 2.4 Metadata Profile Wizard – Repository Selection Window

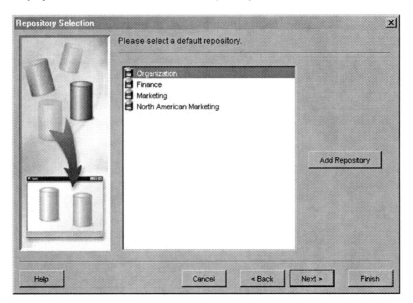

If you are creating a metadata profile for the first time, there are no repositories listed in this window. Click Add Repository to start the New Repository Wizard, which you can use to define a default repository. When creating the first repository, select **Foundation** as the repository type and use the directory that you created when you set up your server (see "Setting Up a SAS Metadata Server" on page 9). For details about creating repositories, see "Creating a Metadata Repository" on page 21.

If you are creating a profile on a server for which you have already defined repositories in SAS Management Console, select one of the defined repositories to use as the default for this profile.

Click Next to continue.

7 The Finish window presents a review of the information you specified in the Metadata Profile Wizard. If any of the information is incorrect, click Back to return to the appropriate window to make changes. When all of the information is correct, click Finish to create the profile.

When you complete the New Repository Wizard and the Metadata Profile Wizard, SAS Management Console connects to the metadata server. You can now use the application to create metadata definitions. The server to which you are connected is referred to as the active server.

Connecting to the Metadata Server

When you start SAS Management Console, the application either runs the default metadata profile (if you specified a default profile) or displays the Open a Metadata Profile window to allow you to choose the profile to use.

Display 2.5 Open a Metadata Profile Window

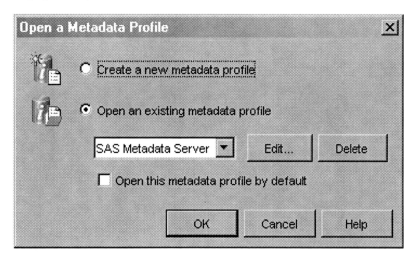

After you select a profile to open, SAS Management Console is connected to the specified SAS Metadata Server. You can begin to create metadata definitions that will be stored in the specified repository.

The status line at the bottom of the SAS Management Console window displays the user ID, machine, and port number of the active server.

The context bar, at the top of the window, displays the repository currently in use. If more than one repository is defined on the current server, you can select another repository from the drop-down list to designate as the active repository.

Using the Error Log

Whenever SAS Management Console encounters an error, it writes the information to the error log file. This file is named errorlog.txt, and is located by default in the SAS Management Console directory.

CHAPTER

3

Managing Metadata

What Is the Metadata Manager?

The Metadata Manager is a SAS Management Console plug-in that enables you to manage metadata definitions by performing the following associated tasks:

metadata repositories
: Add new repositories to the active server, import and export metadata from a repository, change the dependencies for a repository, and perform initialization and cleanup tasks.

metadata servers
: View a list of metadata servers created in the Server Manager plug-in. Note that you cannot use the Metadata Manager plug-in to create new metadata servers.

resource templates
: Add new or updated resource templates to the metadata repository or delete templates that have already been loaded.

job definitions
: Create job definitions to replicate (duplicate without changes) or promote (duplicate with changes) metadata repositories.

Working with Metadata Repositories

The Metadata Manager plug-in lets you work with metadata repositories on the active server. The active server is the metadata server to which SAS Management Console is currently connected and receiving metadata. To manage repositories on a different metadata server, you must disconnect from the active server and use a metadata profile to connect to another server.

Types of Metadata Repositories

You can use the Metadata Manager to create three types of metadata repositories:

Foundation   specifies a stand-alone repository that does not depend on any other repository.

Project   specifies a repository that is dependent on another repository and is used to isolate changes from a production environment.

Custom   specifies a repository that must be dependent on a foundation or custom repository.

Repositories can be associated with one another by dependency relationships. A repository that is dependent upon another repository inherits metadata from the repository on which it is dependent. For example, if Repository B is dependent on Repository A, then Repository B is able to use and access the metadata definitions in Repository A. This capability lets you create a distributed metadata environment, in which all repositories on a server have access to the metadata definitions on the repositories on which they depend.

For example, see the repository configuration in the following figure.

Figure 3.1 Repository Dependency Example

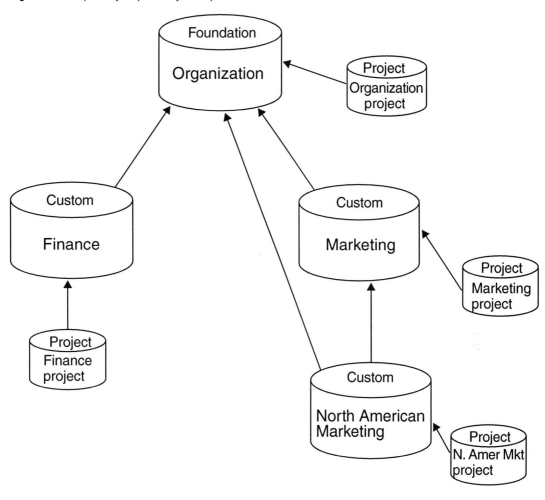

Note: Although the Metadata Manager provides the flexibility for you to set up repositories in a manner appropriate for your business needs, the following is an overview of the repository structure in a typical distributed metadata environment. △

In Figure 3.1 on page 19, the repository named Organization is a foundation repository on the metadata server. This repository stores global metadata, which is the metadata definitions and resource templates that are used throughout the metadata server. The other repositories that you define on this server will be dependent on the foundation repository, which means that they will use the resource templates, user definitions, and permissions and groups that are on the foundation repository, rather than defining their own. Storing this global metadata on a single foundation repository improves metadata integrity and eases maintenance. All changes to the global metadata can be made at a single location, and all dependent repositories are assured of accessing the same global metadata definitions. In this case, the metadata definitions stored in the Organization repository are used throughout the company.

Next, you might define one or more custom repositories that are dependent on the foundation repository. In this example, these are identified as Finance, Marketing, and North American Marketing. These repositories have access to the definitions in the foundation repository but can also contain their own definitions. For example, the Finance repository would contain definitions that are unique to the Finance division. If you want the definitions in each custom repository to be accessible from the other custom repositories, you must create dependencies between the custom repositories as well. However, you cannot create circular dependencies (for example, Custom A depends on Custom B and Custom B depends on Custom A). In this example, the North American Marketing repository needs to access the definitions in the Marketing repository, so there is a dependency relationship between the repositories.

Finally, you would define a project repository for each foundation and custom repository you defined. In this example, the project repositories are Organization Project, Finance Project, Marketing Project, and North American Project. The project repositories are development environments, and are meant to provide an area where you can make and test metadata changes before pushing them to the parent repository. For clarity in the example, the dependencies between the project repositories and the Organization foundation repository are not shown.

Another example of a repository configuration is shown in the following figure.

Figure 3.2 Repository Organization in a Solutions Environment

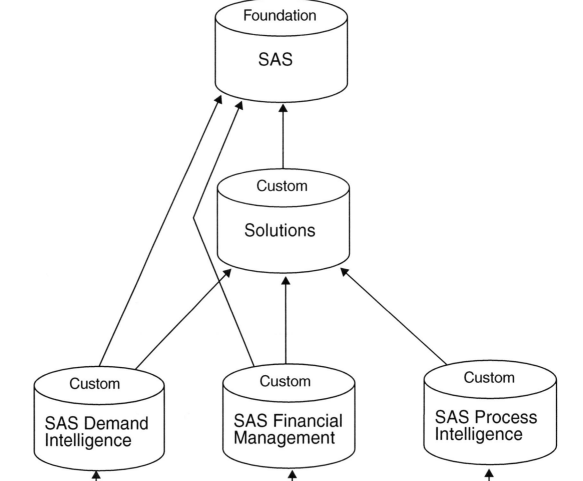

In Figure 3.2 on page 20, the foundation repository contains metadata definitions for all SAS applications. A custom repository named Solutions contains definitions that are common to all installed SAS solutions. Below the Solutions repository are individual custom repositories for each installed SAS solution, each containing definitions that are unique to that solution. Because the repository for each individual solution is dependent on the Solutions repository as well as the SAS repository, each solution has access to the definitions that are applicable to all solutions and to all SAS applications. Finally, a project repository is defined for each solution repository to provide an environment for making changes to the metadata. You could also define project repositories for the SAS and Solutions repositories.

Note: Before you define an environment that uses dependent repositories, you must make sure that the application for which you are creating the environment supports dependent repositories. △

Creating a Metadata Repository

To create a new metadata repository on the active server using the New Repository Wizard:

1 From the navigation tree, select and expand the Metadata Manager, and then select the active server object.

2 From the menu bar, select **Actions ▶ Add Repository** You can also select the option from the pop-up menu or from the toolbar.

The Select Repository Type window of the New Repository Wizard appears.

3 In the Select Repository Type window, choose the type of repository you want to create. The three choices are **Foundation**, **Project**, and **Custom**.

A foundation repository is a repository that is not dependent on any other repository. A project repository is dependent upon a foundation or custom repository, and is used to isolate development work. In practice, the project repository uses the metadata definitions from the parent repository, with users checking out definitions required for project work. A custom repository must also be defined as a dependent repository, but cannot be assigned an owner, as can be done with project repositories.

The first repository you create on a metadata server must be a foundation repository. If no repositories are present on a server, only the **Foundation** radio button is available.

Display 3.1 New Repository Wizard – Select Repository Type Window

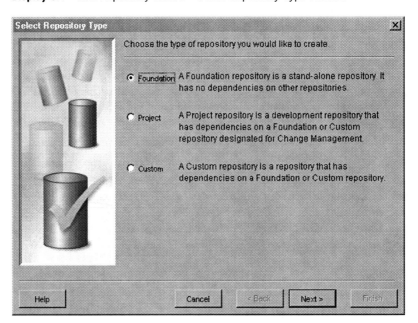

Click Next to continue.

4 In the General Information window, enter a name and, optionally, a description for the repository. Names for foundation and custom repositories can be up to 60 characters in length. However, names for project repositories can only be up to 52 characters in length, because the string "Project:" automatically precedes the name you supply. Click Next to continue.

Display 3.2 New Repository Wizard – General Information Window

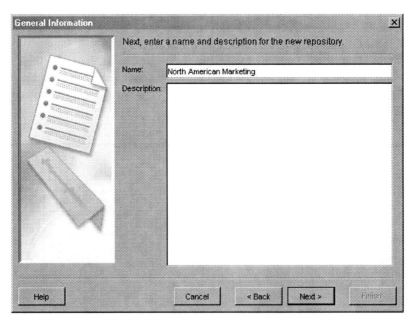

5 In the Definition of Data Source window, select the engine for the server, which specifies the database engine used to access the metadata in the repository. If the server uses SAS, select **Base** for the engine.

Display 3.3   New Repository Wizard – Definition of Data Source Window

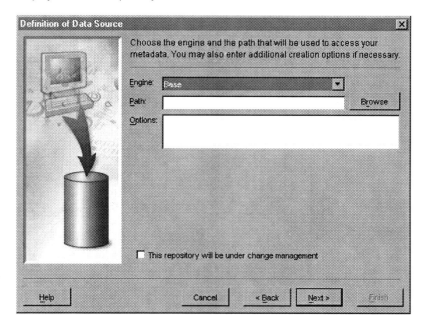

If you select **Base** in the **Engine** field, you must also specify the path for the repository in the **Path** field. If SAS Management Console is running on the same machine where the metadata server is running, you can click Browse to choose the path interactively. You must have full access to the system for the repository directory. For more information about setting system permissions, see *SAS Intelligence Platform: Installation Guide*. Specify other SAS options in the **Options** field (up to 200 characters).

If you select **DB2** or **Oracle** in the **Engine** field, the **Options** field contains a set of default options for each engine.

Specify whether the repository is to be managed by the Change Management Facility. If the repository is under change management, the metadata is subject to check-in and check-out controls and may be updated only by authorized users.

Click Next to continue.

6 If you selected project or custom as the repository type, use the Define Repository Dependencies window to select the repositories on which the new repository will be dependent. Use the arrow controls to move repositories from the **All repositories** list to the **Repository will depend on** list.

Display 3.4   New Repository Wizard – Define Repository Dependencies Window

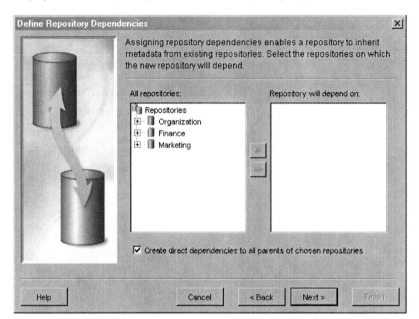

After a dependency is created, the new repository inherits the initialization information from the source of the dependency. A dependency also permits the metadata objects in the new repository to refer to objects in the repository that it is depended upon.

If you are creating a project or custom repository, you must specify a dependency to one existing repository. A custom repository cannot be dependent on a project repository, and a project repository cannot be dependent on another project repository. If the repository to which you create a dependency is itself dependent on another repository, the new repository is dependent on both repositories. However, if you select to create direct dependencies, a direct dependency is established to both the selected parent repository and any parents of the selected repository.

Click ⌷Next⌷ to continue.

7 If you selected project as the repository type, use the Choose Repository Owner window to select the user or group for which the repository is to be created. The list of possible owners is taken from the users and groups defined for the repository upon which the new repository is dependent.

Click ⌷Next⌷ to continue.

Display 3.5 New Repository Wizard – Choose Repository Owner Window

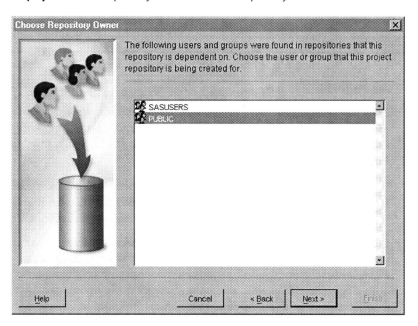

8 Use the Current Settings window to review the information you provided in the wizard. If you need to make changes, click $\boxed{\text{Back}}$ to return to the appropriate window. Click $\boxed{\text{Finish}}$ to close the wizard and create the repository.

Importing Metadata

If your site has already existing metadata, you can import that metadata into a SAS Metadata Repository using SAS Management Console. The basic SAS Management Console install supports importing from the Common Warehouse Metamodel (CWM) format. You can add additional import formats by installing the SAS Metadata Bridges. To obtain the SAS Metadata Bridges, go to **http://support.sas.com/metabridges** or contact your SAS Account Executive. If you installed the SAS Metadata Bridges for metadata export, the formats are already available for the import function.

You can only import relational data (for example, from a SAS library or a DBMS schema). The import process ignores any non-relational data. The following table lists the object types that are imported.

Table 3.1 Imported Object Types

Object type	Description
CWMRDB.Schema	Database schema
CWMRDB.Table	Physical table
CWMRDB.View	
CWMRDB.Column	Column
CWMRDB:SQLDistinctType	UniqueKey
CWMRDB:SQLSimpleType	
CWMRDB:PrimaryKey	UniqueKey
CWMRDBUniqueConstant	

Object type	Description
CWMRDB:ForeignKey	ForeignKey (and associated KeyAssociation)
CWMRDB:SQLIndex	Index

To import metadata:

1 From the navigation tree, select the Metadata Manager and then the active server. Select the repository into which you want to import the metadata and select **Actions ▶ Import Metadata** from the menu bar to open the Metadata Import Wizard.

2 If you have not installed the import and export formats provided by the SAS Metadata Bridges, a message appears to remind you where you can obtain the software. You can choose to not display the message again. Click ⌐OK⌐ to continue.

3 In the Select an Import Format window, select the format of the metadata to be imported. If you have not installed the SAS Metadata Bridges, only CWM Import is available. Click ⌐Show Details⌐ to view detailed information about the selected format type, which includes information such as procedures for generating the file to be imported in the source application, information about the file type required, and answers to frequently asked questions. Click ⌐Next⌐ to continue.

Display 3.6 Metadata Import Wizard – Select an Import Format Window

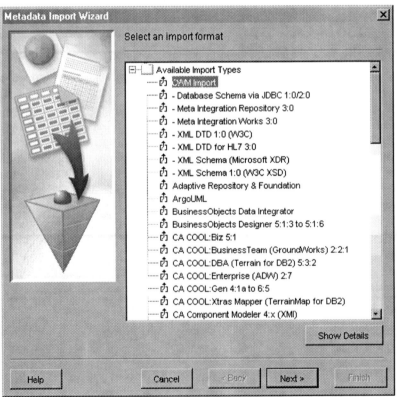

4 In the Select External File window, specify the path and filename of the file that contains the metadata to be imported. Click ⌐Browse⌐ to choose the location interactively. Click ⌐Next⌐ to continue.

Display 3.7   Metadata Import Wizard – Select External File Window

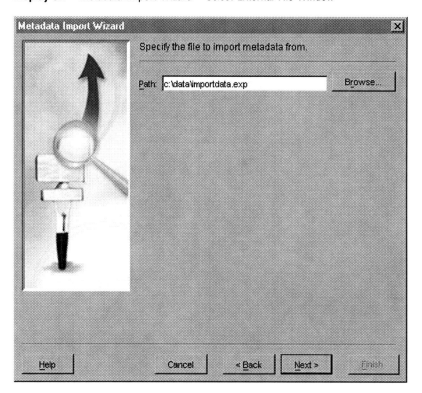

5 If you selected a SAS Metadata Bridges import format type, the Select Bridge Options window might appear. The window does not appear for all import format types. The window lists all of the valid options for the import format and the default values. To change a value, select the value you want to change, then specify the new value. You select values from a drop-down list for some options and type in the desired values for other options. To view Help for an option, position the mouse pointer over the option name to display a brief option description.

If you are importing data that contains double-byte character set data, you must set the **Encoding** option to **UTF8** in this window. If the format you selected does not include an encoding option, you must either select a different format or use other methods to convert the data you want to import to CWM format and then use the Metadata Import Wizard to import the CWM file.

Click Next to continue.

Display 3.8 Metadata Import Wizard – Select Bridge Options Window

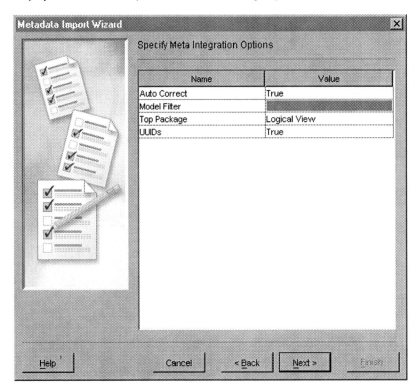

6 In the Select Data Server window, select the data server with which the imported metadata should be associated. A database or SAS server is required if you are importing metadata from a source other than a SAS data source. The data server allows the imported metadata to be linked to the actual data that the metadata describes. Select a server from the drop-down list of defined database servers and SAS servers. Click New to start the New Server Wizard, which you can use to define a new server. Click Next to continue.

Display 3.9 Metadata Import Wizard – Select Data Server Window

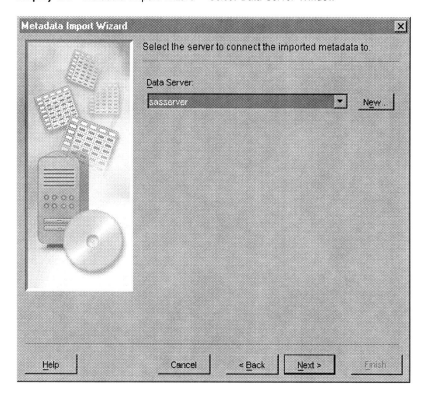

7 If you selected a SAS server or a SAS/SHARE server from the Select Data Server window, the Select SAS Library window appears. Use this window to specify a SAS library that is used to access the imported metadata. Use the **SAS Library** drop-down list to choose from the SAS libraries defined for the selected SAS server. Click New to start the New Library Wizard, which you can use to define a new library. The **Libref** and **Path** fields specify the location of the library. To change these values, click Edit, which displays the properties window for the selected library. Click Next to continue.

Display 3.10 Metadata Import Wizard – Select SAS Library Window

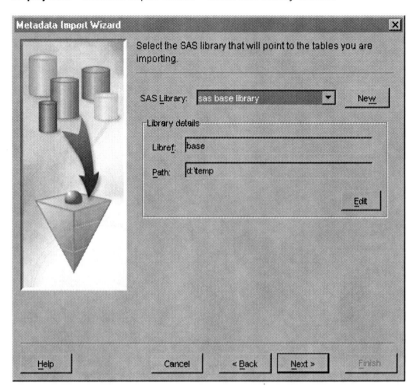

8 If you selected a database server in the Select Data Server window, the Select SAS Server window appears. The server that you select will be used to access the imported metadata. Select a server from the list of all defined SAS servers. Click Next to continue.

Display 3.11   Metadata Import Wizard – Select SAS Server Window

9 The Wizard Finish window displays all of the information specified in the wizard. To make changes, click Back until you reach the appropriate window. If all of the information is correct, click Finish to import the selected metadata.

Exporting Metadata

If your site needs to use the metadata from a SAS Metadata Repository in another type of repository or application, you can export the repository's metadata to a file. The export function exports the entire contents of a repository (other than dependent data) to an export file. The basic SAS Management Console install supports exporting to the Common Warehouse Metamodel (CWM) format. You can add additional export formats by installing the SAS Metadata Bridges. To obtain the SAS Metadata Bridges, go to **http://support.sas.com/metabridges** or contact your SAS Account Executive. If you installed the SAS Metadata Bridges for metadata import, the formats are already available for the export function.

There are two restrictions on the export function:

□ Only relational data is exported (for example, data from a SAS library or a DBMS schema). The following table lists the object types that are exported.

Table 3.2   Exported Object Types

Object type	Description
CWMRDB.Schema	Database schema
CWMRDB.Table	Physical table
CWMRDB.View	
CWMRDB.Column	Column

Object type	Description
CWMRDB:SQLDistinctType	UniqueKey
CWMRDB:SQLSimpleType	
CWMRDB:PrimaryKey	UniqueKey
CWMRDBUniqueConstant	
CWMRDB:ForeignKey	ForeignKey (and associated KeyAssociation)
CWMRDB:SQLIndex	Index

□ If you are exporting metadata from a dependent repository, metadata is not retrieved from the parents of the repository. For example, only tables that use library definitions in the exported repository are exported. Tables that use library definitions in a parent repository are not exported.

To export metadata:

1 From the navigation tree, select the Metadata Manager and then the active server. Select the repository whose metadata you want to export, and select **Actions ▶ Export Metadata** from the menu bar to open the Metadata Export Wizard.

2 If you have not installed the import and export formats provided by the Meta Integration Model Bridge software, a message appears to remind you where you can obtain the software. You can choose to not display the message again. Click OK to continue.

3 In the Select an Export Format window, select the format in which the metadata is to be exported. If you have not installed the SAS Metadata Bridges, only **CWM Export** is available. Click Show Details to view detailed information about the selected format type, which includes information such as procedures for loading the exported file into the target application, information about the file type generated, and answers to frequently asked questions. Click Next to continue.

Display 3.12 Metadata Export Wizard – Select an Export Format Window

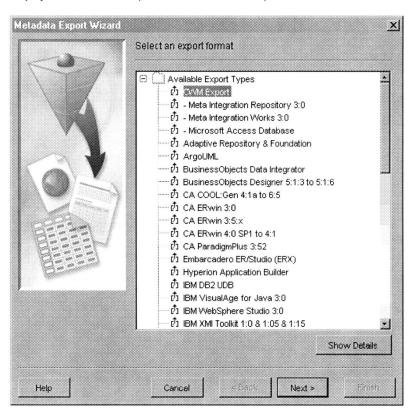

4 In the Select File for Metadata Export window, specify the path and filename of the file into which the metadata should be exported. Click Browse to choose the location interactively. Click Next to continue.

Display 3.13 Metadata Export Wizard – Select File for Metadata Export Window

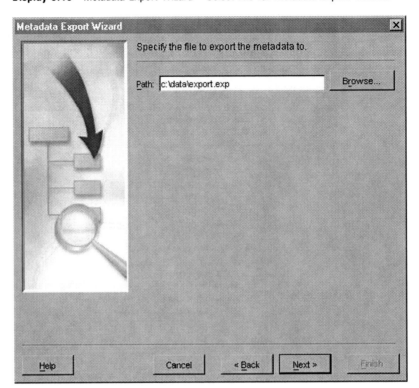

5 If you selected a SAS Metadata Bridges export format type, the Select Bridge Options window might appear. The window does not appear for all export format types. The window lists all of the valid options for the export format and the default values. To change a value, select the value you want to change, then specify the new value. You select values from a drop–down list for some options and type in the desired values for other options. To view Help for an option, position the mouse pointer over the option name to display a brief option description.

If you are exporting data that contains double-byte character set data, you must set the **Encoding** option to **UTF8** in this window. If the format you selected does not include an encoding option, you must either select a different format or export the data to a CWM file and then convert the data using other methods.

Click Next to continue.

Display 3.14 Metadata Export Wizard – Bridge Options Window

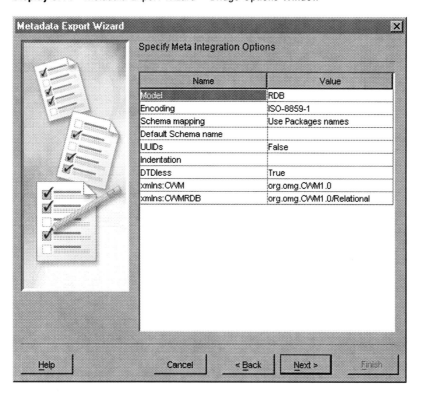

6 The Wizard Finish window displays all of the information specified in the wizard. To make changes, click $\boxed{\text{Back}}$ until you reach the appropriate window. If all of the information is correct, click $\boxed{\text{Finish}}$ to export the selected metadata.

Changing Repository Dependencies

After you create a repository, you can change or add to the list of repositories upon which the new repository is dependent.

To change repository dependencies:

1 In the navigation tree, select the Metadata Manager plug-in and the active server.

2 In the navigation tree or display area, select the repository whose dependencies you want to change and select **Actions ▶ Edit Dependencies** from the menu bar. The Edit Dependencies window appears.

Display 3.15 Edit Dependencies Window

3 The window contains two lists. Repositories that are defined on the active server and that can establish a valid dependency with the selected server are listed in the **All repositories** list. For example, if you are changing the dependencies for a project repository, the **All repositories** list contains the foundation repository and any change managed custom repositories. The repositories upon which the selected repository is dependent are listed in the **Depends on** list.

To add a dependency to a repository, select the repository in the **All repositories** list and use the arrow control to move the repository to the **Depends on** list.

To remove a dependency, select the repository in the **Depends on** list and use the arrow control to move the repository to the **All repositories** list.

4 When you create a dependency, you also create a dependency to all of the parents of the selected repository unless you deselect the create direct dependencies option. For example, if you specify that repository A should be dependent on repository B, and repository B is already dependent on repositories C and D, then repository A is dependent on repositories B, C, and D.

5 Click ‾O‾K‾ to close the window and create the dependencies.

Maintaining the Active Server

The Metadata Manager plug-in provides several functions for maintaining the active server and the repositories on the server. The functions available are the following:

Delete   deletes the selected repository, the repository contents, and all metadata that defines the repository. To select this function, select the repository you want to delete under the active server and select **Delete** from the pop-up menu.

Unregister   deletes the metadata that defines the selected repository, but leaves the repository contents intact. You cannot access an unregistered repository from the current metadata server until you register the repository again. To select this function, select the repository you want to unregister under the active server and select **Unregister** from the pop-up menu or the **Actions** menu.

Purge permanently removes all metadata items that have been marked for deletion in the selected repository. To select this function, select the repository whose contents you want to purge under the active server and select **Purge** from the pop-up menu or the **Actions** menu.

Format formats the selected repository, which removes all metadata currently in the repository. To select this function, select the repository you want to format under the active server and select **Format** from the pop-up menu or the **Actions** menu.

Truncate deletes all of the metadata objects in the selected repository, but does not delete the object containers or remove the repository registration. To select this function, select the repository you want to truncate under the active server and select **Truncate** from the pop-up menu or the **Actions** menu.

Initialize **Repository** redefines initial settings for the repository, including user groups and permissions, access control templates, and installed resource templates. To select this function, select the repository you want to initialize under the active server and select **Initialize Repository** from the pop-up menu or the **Actions** menu.

If you format and then initialize a change–managed repository, the change management will no longer be applied. To restore change management, you must unregister and re-register the repository. In the process of re-registering the repository, you can activate change management in the New Repository Wizard. See "Unregistering and Re-registering Repositories" on page 37 for more information.

This function is not available for project repositories.

Stop stops the active server. To select this function, select the active server and select **Stop** from the pop-up menu or from the **Actions** menu.

Pause pauses all repositories on the active server. To select this function, select the active server and select **Pause** from the pop-up menu or from the **Actions** menu.

Resume resumes operation for a paused server. To select this function, select the active server and select **Resume** from the pop-up menu or from the **Actions** menu.

Unregistering and Re-registering Repositories

Unregistering a repository is the process of removing metadata that describes the repository without altering the contents of the repository itself. An unregistered repository is invisible to the metadata server. Re-registering a repository is the process of defining a repository while specifying the same metadata that was removed, making the repository visible to the metadata server.

When performing this procedure, it is important that you make careful note of all of the repository's attributes before you unregister it. When you use the New Repository Wizard to re-register the repository, you must specify all options exactly as they were. The repository path must be identical in order for the repository to access any existing metadata objects. If the repository type is different, the repository is initialized upon creation, and any existing metadata definitions may be lost. For example, if the unregistered repository was a foundation repository, re-register it as a foundation repository; if it was a custom repository, re-register it as a custom repository.

To unregister a repository:

1 From the Metadata Manager in the navigation tree, expand the Active Server and select the repository you want to unregister.

2 Select **Properties** from the pop-up menu or the **File** menu. In the Properties window, select the Registration tab and make note of the path specified in the **Location** field and the engine type specified in the **Engine** field. You must have this information in order to re-register the repository. If you do not specify the same path and engine type, the repository is created as a new repository, rather than a re-registered repository. Close the Properties window.

3 With the repository still selected, select **Unregister** from the pop-up menu or the **Actions** menu.

4 A confirmation dialog appears. Click OK to unregister the repository.

To re-register a repository:

1 From the Metadata Manager in the navigation tree, select the Active Server and select **Add Repository** from the pop-up menu, the **Actions** menu, or the toolbar.

2 The New Repository Wizard starts and guides you through the process of creating a new repository.

3 When specifying the repository type, verify that the type you specify is identical to the type of the repository you want to re-register. If the repository types do not match, the repository will be initialized when it is created and all metadata definitions in the repository might be lost.

4 Verify that the engine type and the path for the repository are the same as the repository you unregistered. The path must be identical in order for the re-registered repository to contain any existing metadata definitions.

5 Finish entering all information in the New Repository Wizard, then use the **Repository** drop-down list to specify the re-registered repository as the active repository. Verify that the metadata definitions are intact.

Managing Resource Templates

Resource templates are XML files that define how SAS Management Console defines a particular type of metadata object. The template for a specific object (for example, a SAS workspace server) specifies the specific information that SAS Management Console requests when defining the object and the information that is displayed for the object's properties. Because each metadata object uses a separate definition, you only have to load an updated resource template to change the information needed to define a particular object.

A full set of resource templates is loaded whenever you create a foundation metadata repository, and it is strongly recommended that you do not load resource templates into any other type of repository on a metadata server. Any project or custom repositories that are dependent on the foundation repository are able to access the foundation repository's resource templates.

To delete a resource template, select the Resource Templates folder under the Metadata Manager in the navigation tree, select the template you want to delete in the display area, and select **Delete** from the pop-up menu, the **Edit** menu, or the toolbar.

Adding Resource Templates

Although a full set of resource templates is loaded into foundation metadata repositories upon repository creation, there might be instances where you need to load new or updated resource templates. For example, if support is added for a new server type, that server's resource template must be added to the existing set. If the information required to define a particular server changes, then the old template must be deleted and the new one added.

To load resource templates:

1 Ensure that the currently selected repository is a foundation repository. If necessary, select the foundation repository for the active metadata server from the **Repository** drop-down list.

2 From the navigation tree, select the Metadata Manager plug-in and then select the Resource Templates folder.

3 Select **Add Resource Templates** from the **Actions** menu, the pop-up menu, or the toolbar. The Add Resource Template Wizard starts.

4 In the Installation Type window, specify what kind of installation you want to perform.

Display 3.16 Add Resource Template Wizard - Installation Type Window

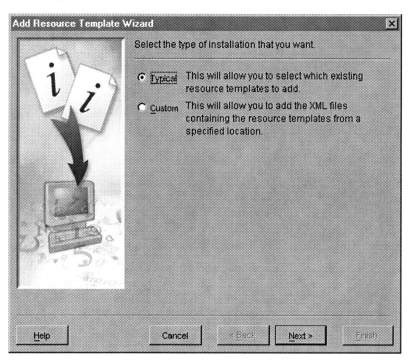

Select **Typical** to load resource templates from the standard location in the SAS Management Console installation directory. Use this option to reload one or more of the default resource templates.

Select **Custom** to install specific resource template files from a specified location. Use this option to load specially created or modified resource templates.

Click Next to continue.

5 If you selected **Typical** as the installation type, the Template Selection window appears. The resource templates are organized into folders and subfolders based

on the type of metadata object each one defines. Open the appropriate folders and select the templates you want to add. Click ⌈Select All⌉ to select all of the resource templates in all of the folders. Click ⌈Next⌉ to continue.

Display 3.17 Add Resource Template Wizard - Template Selection Window

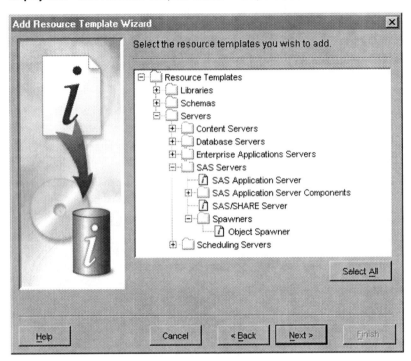

6 If you selected **Custom** as the installation type, the Template Location window appears.

Display 3.18 Add Resource Template Wizard - Template Location Window

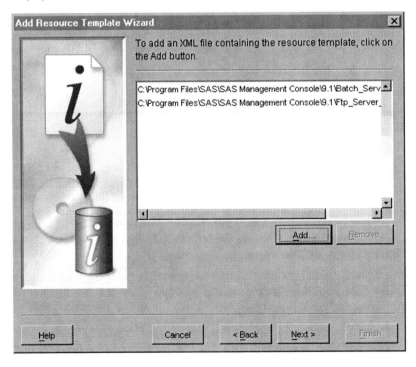

To specify the location of a resource template XML file, click Add and use the file browser that appears to locate the file. To remove a template file from the list in the Template Location window, select the filename and click Remove. Click Next to continue.

7 If you selected **Typical** as the installation type, the Locale window appears. The locale specifies the language in which the resource template appears.

Display 3.19 Add Resource Template Wizard - Locale Window

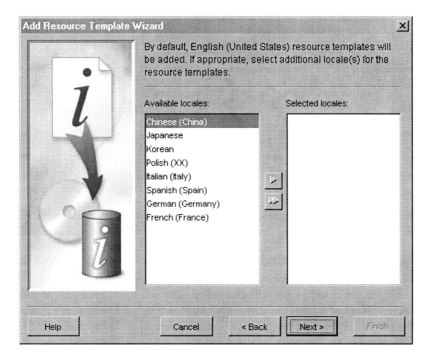

Use the arrow buttons to move locales from the **Available locales** list to the **Selected locales** list. Templates for the English locale are automatically installed. Click Next to continue.

8 The Finish window displays all of the information specified in the wizard. To make changes, click Back until you reach the appropriate window. If all of the information is correct, click Finish to load the selected resource templates. If the currently selected repository is not a foundation repository, a warning message appears to confirm that you want to add the resource templates to a dependent repository.

Replicating and Promoting Metadata

SAS Management Console provides the ability to copy the contents of a metadata repository to another repository. If the contents are copied without any changes, the process is referred to as replication. If the copying process includes the ability to change metadata values, the process is called promotion. SAS Management Console also lets you save the promotion or replication process you define as a job, which lets you rerun the process at any time without having to redefine the process parameters. However, the substitutions in a promotion job are not dynamic, so if you make any changes to a repository that has been promoted, you must create a new job definition.

Promotion and replication must be between servers running on the same platform. For example, promotion between two Windows servers is allowed, but promotion between a UNIX server and a Windows server is not allowed.

You should only promote or replicate foundation and custom repositories. Project repositories should not be promoted or replicated.

As an example of using the promotion and replication functions, consider the environment shown in the following figure.

Figure 3.3 Development, Testing, and Production Environment

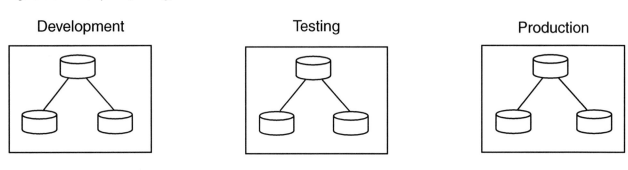

In this example, an organization has created three metadata servers and corresponding repositories to provide a development area, testing area, and production area, as shown in Figure 3.3 on page 42. System administrators use the development server to create new metadata definitions and verify their function in the development environment. Prior to making the development changes, a replication job is created and run to copy the current metadata on the Production server to the Testing server and another replication job is created and run to copy the metadata from the Testing server to the Development server (Figure 3.4 on page 42). These jobs ensure that all three servers are using the same environment. Note that the replication process creates repositories with identical names on the target servers. A new replication or promotion job will not run if the target server already contains a repository with the same name as the repository being promoted or replicated.

Figure 3.4 Production to Testing Replication

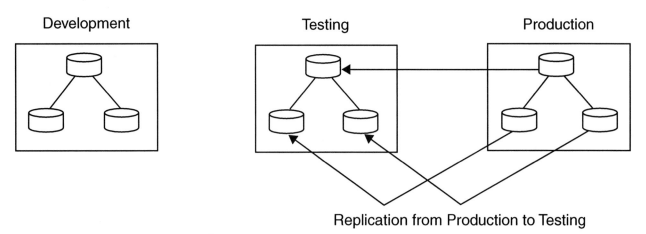

Next, a promotion job is created and run to copy the development metadata to the testing environment, as shown in Figure 3.5 on page 43.

Figure 3.5 Development to Testing Promotion

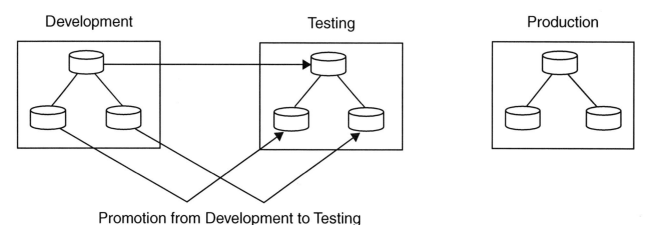

Promotion from Development to Testing

The promotion job changes the parameters in the development metadata such as server names and port numbers in order to make it applicable for the testing environment. Because the promotion job is saved, it can easily be run whenever metadata needs to be promoted from development to testing.

After the definitions are tested, another promotion job is run to promote the tested metadata back to the production server, as shown in Figure 3.6 on page 43.

Figure 3.6 Testing to Production Promotion

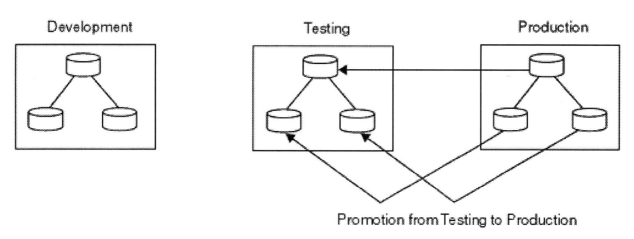

Promotion from Testing to Production

Promoting Dependent Repositories

If you are promoting a dependent repository, the set of parent repositories must be present on both the source and the target servers. The promotion process uses the permissions that are defined in the server's foundation repository and inherited by the dependent repository.

To promote a dependent repository:

1 Replicate all parent repositories of the dependent repository from the source server to the target server.

2 Replicate the dependent repository that you want to promote.

3 On the target server, define the dependency relationship between the dependent repository and its parents. The repository and dependency structure should now be identical between the source server and target server.

4 Promote the dependent repository from the source to the target server.

You must follow this procedure before you promote a dependent repository for the first time. The dependency relationships remain in place for subsequent promotion jobs. However, if the dependency structure changes on the source server, you must follow the procedure again to establish an equivalent dependency structure on the target server.

Working With User Macros

During the running of a promotion or replication job, several user macros are called and processed if they have been defined. These macros enable you to perform additional processing during the promotion or replication process. See Appendix 1, "Replication and Promotion Macros," on page 157 for a list of the macros that you can specify.

Running Replication and Promotion Jobs

In order to create and run replication and promotion jobs, you must first configure the these environments:

□ a source environment

□ a target environment

□ an administration environment

To configure each environment, you must define a metadata server, a metadata repository, and other specific servers and users. After you have configured the required environments, you can use the Replication Wizard and Promotion Wizard to create and run replication and promotion jobs.

For detailed information on configuring the replication and promotion environments and defining and running jobs, see *SAS Intelligence Platform: System Administration Guide*.

Upgrading Repository Metadata

The Upgrade Metadata function enables you to apply changes to the metadata repositories required by new releases of SAS. Because the changes are applied to all repositories on the active server, you must be an unrestricted user in order to run the utility.

To update the repositories on the active server, follow these steps:

1 In the navigation tree, select the active server.

2 Select **Upgrade Metadata** from the pop-up menu.

   If the user is not specifically defined as an unrestricted user, an error message appears and the repositories are not updated.

3 If the user is defined as an unrestricted user, the updates are applied to all repositories on the active server.

   If the repositories have already been upgraded, the message "All repositories up-to-date" appears.

   When the process is complete, the message "The metadata server has been successfully updated" appears.

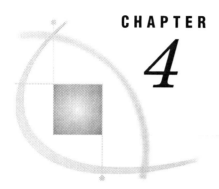

CHAPTER

4

Managing Users

What Is the User Manager?

The User Manager is a SAS Management Console plug-in that provides functions to manage metadata definitions for users and groups of users. Each user and group that accesses secure resources on a SAS Metadata Server must be represented by an identity on the server. Individual users are represented by Person objects, and groups are represented by IdentityGroup objects. You must also create user definitions for logins needed when creating object spawner definitions or setting up load balancing.

Planning for Users and Groups

Before you begin defining users and groups, you must formulate a strategy for deciding which groups will be created, which users will belong to those groups, and which individual users will need to be defined. Refer to *SAS Intelligence Platform: Security Administration Guide* for information about planning for users and groups.

The user definitions you will need to create are either individual users with specialized access requirements (most of whom will be organized into groups) or specialized functional logins (such as for operator connections to spawners or for spawner-to-spawner connections in load balancing).

For ease of maintenance, you should minimize the user definitions that are not in groups. For example, assume that your site has three administrator IDs that have identical access requirements. If you define the administrators as individual users, you must give each administrator authorization to access each metadata object individually. Later, if you need to add another administrator, you must go back to each object and authorize the new administrator to access each definition. However, if you begin by creating an administrator group that is made up of the administrator user definitions, you only need to create a user definition for the new administrator and add the definition to the administrator group in order to give the new administrator the same access.

When planning for groups, you must consider grouping users that need to access restricted metadata. SAS Management Console uses two general groups for users for which you do not have to specify members:

PUBLIC   implicitly contains all users who can authenticate to the metadata server. The access rules you define for the PUBLIC group apply to all users that are not members of a group (although you can override these rules).

SASUSERS   represents all users that are specifically defined in the User Manager with a definition that includes a login.

When planning for groups, first evaluate which resources require restricted access, then ensure that a group exists or is created for the users that need to access each restricted resource. For example, you might want to create a group of users with read and write access to servers and libraries containing salary information. All other users (represented by the PUBLIC group) are denied read and write access to these resources. See *SAS Intelligence Platform: Security Administration Guide* for information about planning for users and groups.

It is strongly suggested that you create all user definitions in the foundation repository of a metadata server, rather than in any dependent repositories. User definitions created in the foundation repository are accessible to all other repositories that are dependent on the foundation repository. Storing user definitions in the foundation repository also keeps the user metadata centralized, rather than spread over multiple repositories. Using centralized metadata simplifies the process of locating and maintaining metadata definitions.

Defining a User

Defining a user involves specifying identifying information about the user and identifying the user's login IDs and authentication domains. A user can only access resources in authentication domains on which the user or a group to which the user belongs has a valid login.

To define a user:

1 Select the User Manager plug-in in the navigation tree and select **New ▶ User**from the pop-up menu or the **Actions** menu, or select the **New User** tool from the toolbar. The New User Properties window appears.

Display 4.1   New User Properties Window – General Tab

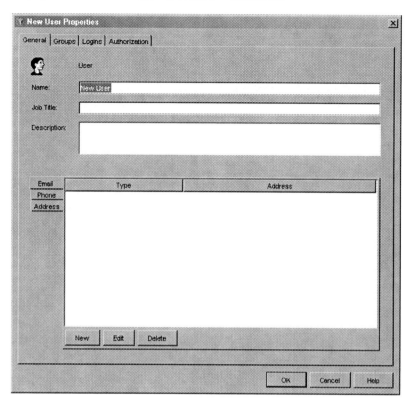

2 The New User Properties window opens with the General tab displayed. Use this tab to specify a name for the user and supply identifying information. Select the Groups tab when you are finished.

3 The Groups tab lets you assign the user to a user group. If you have created any user groups, they are listed in the **Available Groups** list. Select the groups to which the user should belong in the **Available Groups** list, then use the arrow control to move them to the **Member of** list. You can also assign users to groups after the users have been created.

Display 4.2 New User Properties Window – Groups Tab

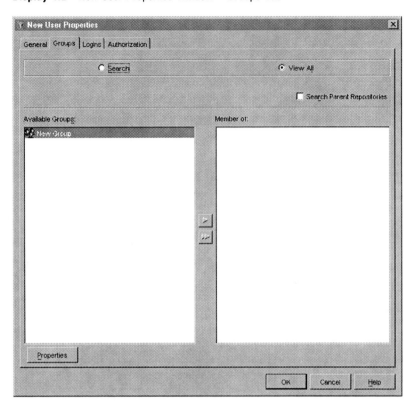

By default, the tab lists all user groups created in the active repository. If the active repository is dependent on another repository, select **Search Parent Repositories** to display a list of the groups on the active repository and any parent repositories. The user can be a member of any of the listed groups, regardless of the groups' location.

Display 4.3 New User Properties Window – Search Parent Repositories

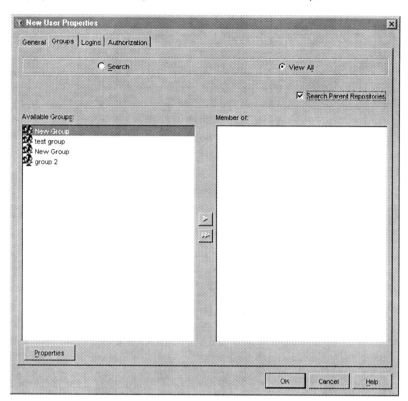

If the repository contains a large number of groups, select the **Search** radio button to display the search fields.

Display 4.4   New User Properties Window – Search for Users

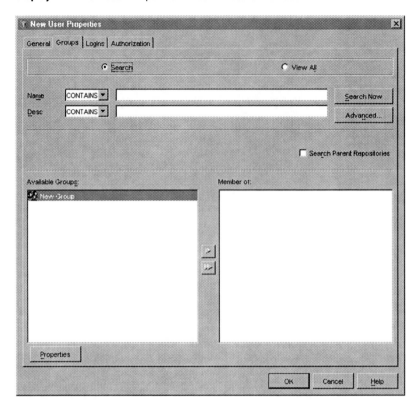

By default, you can search for the name or description of a group. Click
Advanced to search using a user ID.

When you have finished selecting groups for the user, select the Logins tab.

4 The Logins tab allows you to specify all of the login IDs associated with the user.

Display 4.5   New User Properties Window – Logins Tab

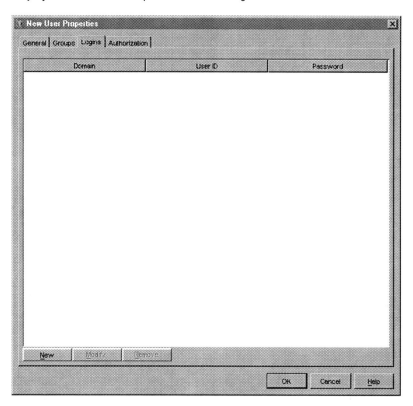

To add a login to the list, click ⌈New⌋. You must specify at least one login for the user in order to create a valid metadata identity.

See *SAS Intelligence Platform: Security Administration Guide* for a detailed explanation of the relationships between logins, authentication domains, and users, as well as information about how a SAS Metadata Server uses logins.

In the New Login Properties window, specify the user ID, password (which you must enter twice for confirmation), and authentication domain for the user's login. You must select the authentication domain that is associated with the server to which the login provides access.

Display 4.6 New Login Properties Window

Click New to specify a new authentication domain if the correct authentication domain is not listed. If you are specifying a login on a Microsoft Windows system, specify the user ID as *domain\userid*. Click OK to return to the Logins tab.

To change or delete a login, select the login and click Modify or Remove.

Make sure you define all possible logins on all authentication domains for the user or a group to which the user belongs.

Although logins can be added after the user has been defined, by default only the administrative user and the person represented by this Person object can add logins. You must grant WriteMetadata permission to a user in order for that user to be able to add logins to his or her Person object.

When you have finished defining all logins for the user, select the Authorization tab.

5 The Authorization tab specifies the users or groups that are granted or denied permission to perform specified actions on the user definition. Click Add to add a user or group to the list of those having specified permissions for the user definition.

Display 4.7 New User Properties Window – Authorization Tab

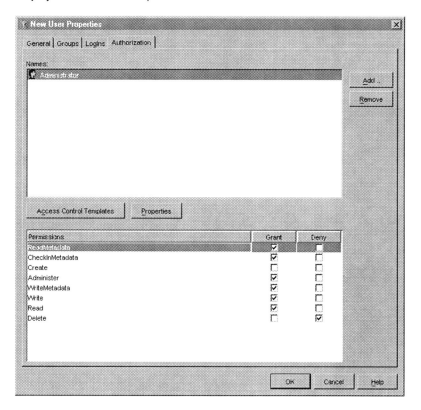

In this example, the Administrator user has been granted permission to read metadata, checkin metadata, administer, read and write, and has been denied permission to delete. All of these permissions are for the access to the user definition, not to the resources accessed by the user.

Unless users are specifically granted WriteMetadata permission for the user definition, only the administrative user and the person represented by the Person object can modify the definition after it has been created.

For a detailed explanation about defining authorization, see Chapter 7, "Managing Authorizations," on page 105.

Note: The Authorization tab for a user definition does not display any inherited permissions. △

6 Click OK to close the New User Properties window and define the user.

Defining a Group

In your organization, you might have resources that you only want to be accessible to certain users. For example, you do not want a server that contains salary information to be accessible to all users, but only to a select group. To implement this type of control, SAS Management Console lets you define groups of users with common access requirements, then specify the access rules that apply to all members of the group.

When a group member attempts to access a restricted resource, the group's permissions for the resource are evaluated. If the group has authorization to access the resource, then the group members also have authorization. Authorization only has to be defined for the group, rather than for each user in the group.

To define a group:

1 From the navigation tree, select the User Manager plug-in and select **New ▶ Group**from the pop-up menu or the **Actions** menu, or select the **New Group** tool from the toolbar. The New Group Properties window appears.

Display 4.8 New Group Properties Window – General Tab

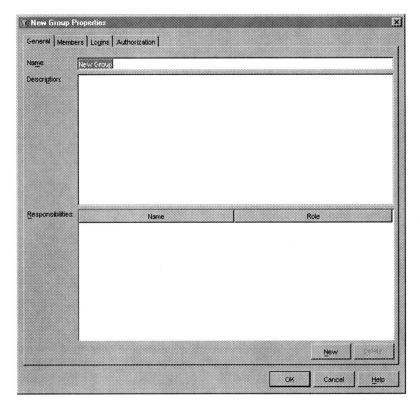

2 The New Group Properties window appears with the General tab displayed. Enter a name, a description, and the users that have owner and administrator responsibilities for the group. The responsibilities are for information purposes only. Access controls for the group are controlled on the Authorization tab. To specify a new responsibility, click New, then select from the defined users in the **Name** column and the responsibility types in the **Role** column. Select the Members tab when you are finished.

3 The Members tab lets you specify the members of the group.

Display 4.9   New User Properties Window – Members Tab

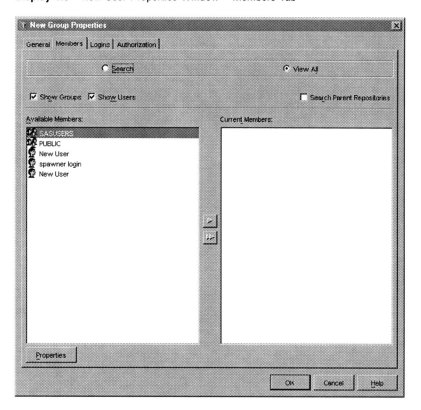

To add individual users or groups to the group being defined, select the users or groups in the **Available Members** list and use the arrow controls to move the entries to the **Current Members** list. Select the **Show Groups** or **Show Users** check boxes to control the entries that are displayed in the **Available Members** list. Select **View All** to see a list of all defined users and groups or select **Search** to find a particular user or group. Select a user or group and click Properties to view detailed information about the selected user or group.

You must be careful when creating groups that contain other groups, because of the potential for creating authorization conflicts.

When you have finished adding group members, select the Logins tab.

4 The Logins tab lets you define shared logins that group members can use to authenticate to servers in other authentication domains. Defining logins for a group is optional.

Display 4.10   New User Properties Window – Logins Tab

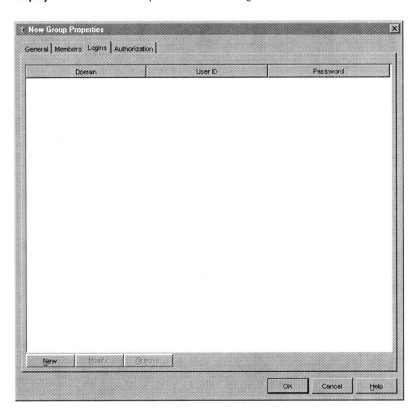

To add a new login for the group, click ⬚New⬚.

In the New Login Properties window, specify the user ID, password (which you must enter twice for confirmation), and authentication domain for the group login.

Display 4.11   New Login Properties Window

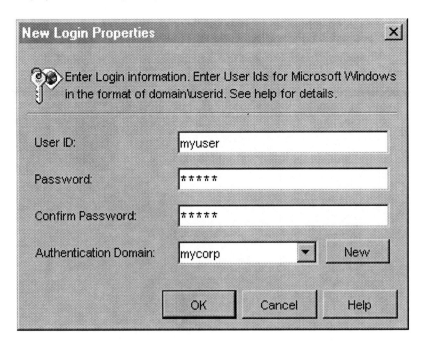

Click [New] to specify a new authentication domain if the correct authentication domain is not listed. If you are specifying a login on a Microsoft Windows system, specify the user ID as *domain\userid*. Click [OK] to return to the Logins tab.

Make sure you define all possible logins on all domains for the group.

Although logins can be added after the group has been defined, only users granted WriteMetadata permission for the IdentityGroup and Login objects can add logins. You must grant WriteMetadata permission to a user in order for that user to be able to add logins to this IdentityGroup object.

When you have finished defining all logins for the group, select the Authorization tab.

5 The Authorization tab specifies the users or groups that are granted or denied permission to perform specified actions on the group definition. Click [Add] to add a user or group to the list of those having specified permissions for the group definition.

Display 4.12   New User Properties Window – Authorization Tab

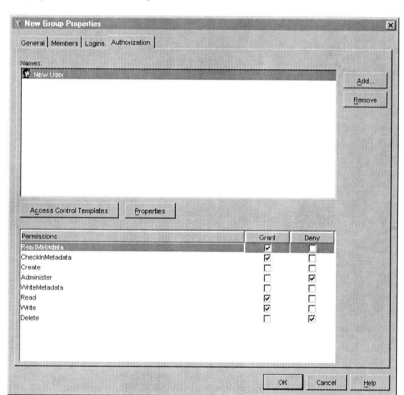

In this example, the user New User has been granted permission to read metadata, checkin metadata, read and write, and has been denied permission to administer and delete. All of these permissions are for the access to the group definition, not to the resources accessed by the group.

For a detailed explanation about defining authorization, see Chapter 7, "Managing Authorizations," on page 105.

6 Click [OK] to close the New Group Properties window and define the group.

5

Managing Servers

What Is the Server Manager?

The Server Manager is a SAS Management Console plug-in that provides the ability to define and manage metadata definitions for servers. The specific types of servers that the plug-in can define are determined by the resource templates that are loaded. Resource templates are XML files that define the information that the plug-in requests for each type of metadata definition. You can specify the servers that your site can install by controlling the server resource templates that are loaded.

You can use the Server Manager to define these types of servers:

content servers	servers that provide content for a Web application (such as the SAS Information Delivery Portal).
database servers	servers that are used to store data that is used by other applications and is stored in a format usable by the applications.
enterprise application servers	servers that are used to run database or analytics applications other than SAS. Users can send requests to the application running on an enterprise application server and have the results returned to them.
SAS servers	servers that are used to run SAS sessions. Users can send requests to the SAS session on the server and receive the results. SAS Management Console supports several types of SAS servers, including metadata servers, workspace servers, stored process servers, and OLAP servers.
spawners	SAS sessions that listen for client requests for server sessions and pass the requests to a SAS server.

<table>
<tr><td>scheduling
servers</td><td>servers needed to support scheduling of jobs from SAS Data Integration Studio or other applications.</td></tr>
</table>

Managing SAS Servers

Before you start defining SAS servers, you should understand how SAS server definitions are organized by the SAS metadata model and presented by SAS Management Console.

Figure 5.1 Organization of SAS Server Definitions

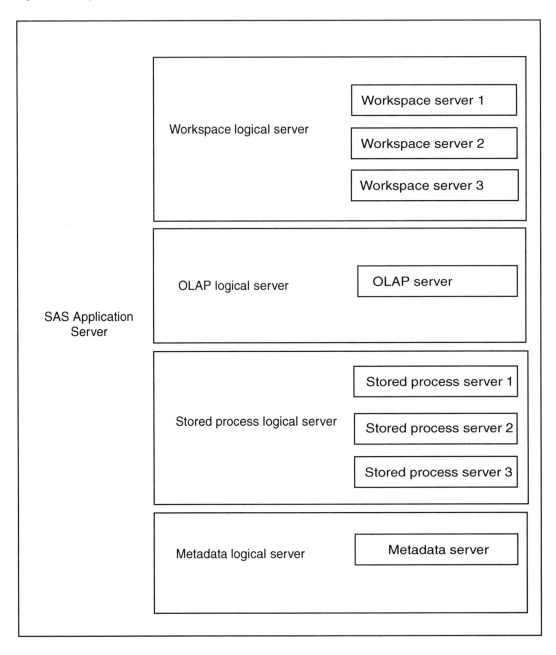

The highest-level server (also known as a server context) is a container for physical servers that should share resources (such as libraries). Within each server are one or more logical servers. A logical server is a grouping of one or more physical servers, or server components. This organization helps in sharing resources. For example, when you define a SAS library in the Data Library Manager, you can assign the library to the server and all of the physical servers within the server will have access to the library. The logical server grouping also makes it easier to set up load balancing or pooling. Each server can only have one logical server of each type.

Defining a Basic SAS Server

To create a new SAS server definition:

1 From the navigation tree, select the Server Manager plug-in. Then select **New Server** from the pop-up menu, toolbar, or **Actions** menu. The New Server Wizard starts.

2 Use the Server Type window to select the server you are defining.

Display 5.1 New Server Wizard – Server Type Window

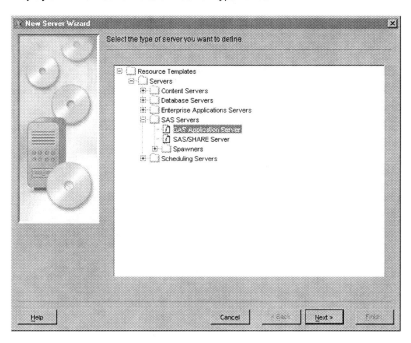

Locate the SAS Servers folder and select **SAS Application Server**. Click Next to continue.

3 In the Name and Description window, specify a name and a description (optional). The name you provide will be the displayed name of the server.

Display 5.2   New Server Wizard – Name and Description Window

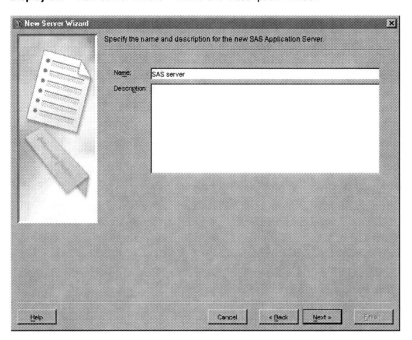

Click Next to continue.

4 The Server Options window lists information about the vendor and version of the server software. Click Next to continue.

5 The SAS Server Type window lists the types of SAS application servers you can define.

Display 5.3   New Server Wizard – SAS Server Type Window

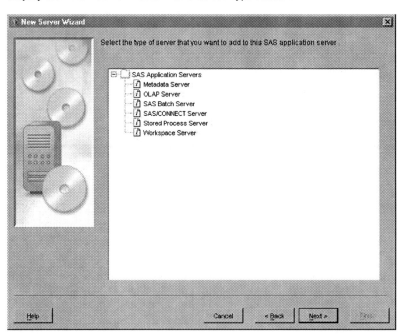

The type you choose will become the first logical server and the first server component in the server. For example, if you select metadata server as the server

type, the server will contain a logical metadata server which in turn contains a metadata server. Click [Next] to continue.

6 Use the SAS Server Configuration window to specify how clients will connect to the server (this window does not appear if you are defining a batch server).

Display 5.4 New Server Wizard – SAS Server Configuration Window

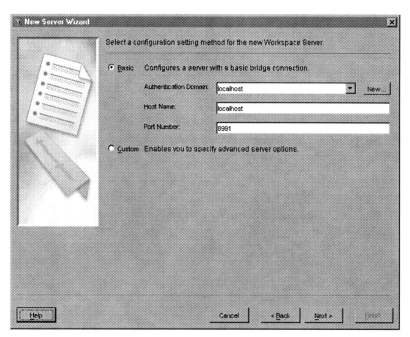

The **Basic** option lets you quickly define an Integrated Object Model (IOM) Bridge connection for the server, using defaults for all connection parameters not listed on this window. Select **Basic** and specify these items:

Authentication Domain	specifies the domain used to authenticate logins to the server. Click [New] to define a new domain.
Host Name	specifies the host machine on which the server runs.
Port Number	specifies the port on the host used for connections between the server and clients.

The **Custom** option lets you define all aspects of an IOM Bridge connection or define a Component Object Model (COM) connection (this type of connection is not available for SAS/CONNECT or batch servers). If you are creating a definition for a server that uses SAS V8.2, you must select **Custom**. See "Defining a SAS V8.2 Server" on page 64 for more information.

Click [Next] to continue. The Finish window displays all of the information you entered in the wizard. If you need to make any changes, click [Back] to return to the appropriate window. If all of the information is correct, click [Finish] to define the server.

7 Open the Server Manager in the navigation tree to see the server you defined.

Display 5.5   Navigation Tree – SAS Server Definition

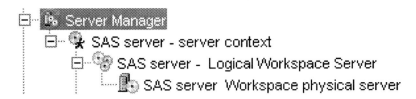

The top-level object under the tree is the SAS application server. Open the SAS server to see the logical server (a logical workspace server in this example). Open the logical server to see the physical server (workspace server in this example).

Defining a SAS V8.2 Server

If you are creating a server definition for a SAS server that uses V8.2, you must specify that the connection to the server not use encryption.

To create a definition for a SAS V8.2 server:

1 Follow the procedure in "Defining a Basic SAS Server" on page 61 until you reach the SAS Server Configuration window (do not select either batch or SAS/CONNECT as the SAS server type). In this window, select **Custom** and click Next.

2 In the Server Options window, specify the information for the specific type of SAS server you selected, then click Next.

Display 5.6   New Server Wizard – Server Options Window

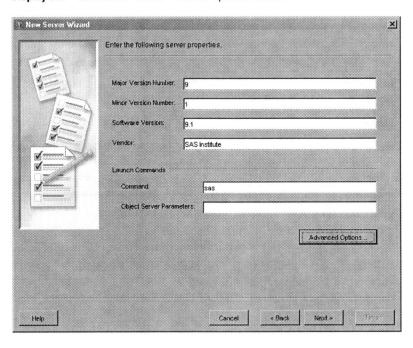

3 In the SAS Connection Type window, select **Bridge Connection** and click Next.

Display 5.7 New Server Wizard – SAS Connection Type Window

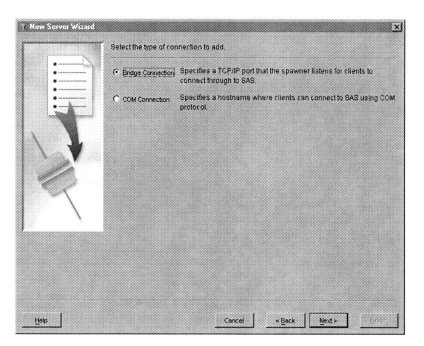

4 In the Connection Options window, specify the requested information, then click **Advanced Options**.

Display 5.8 New Server Wizard – Connection Options Window

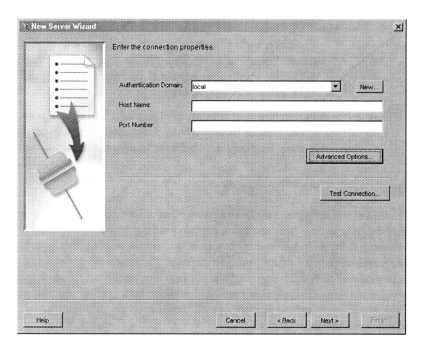

5 In the Advanced Options window, select the Encryption tab.

6 On the Encryption tab, select a value of **None** from the Required Encryption Level drop-down list.

Display 5.9 Bridge Connection Advanced Options Window

7 Click OK in the Advanced Options window, then click Next in the Connection Options window to go to the Finish window and complete the server definition.

Adding to the SAS Server

After you have created a SAS server, including the logical server, you can add the following to the server definitions:

server component
: Within the server, you can add a different type of SAS server, along with its corresponding logical server.

server
: Within a logical server, you can add a new physical server of the same type. For example, within a logical workspace server, you can add new workspace servers. Metadata and OLAP logical servers can only contain a single server.

connection
: For a physical server, you can add another connection of a different type. For example, if you defined an IOM Bridge connection to a server, you can add a COM connection.

Adding a SAS Server Component

Adding server components is the process of adding additional types of SAS servers (consisting of a logical server and a corresponding physical server) to a server. All of the server components in a server can share resources and definitions for objects such as libraries and database schemas. You can only add server components that are not already present in a SAS application server. For example, if an application server contains a workspace logical server and a metadata logical server, you cannot add another workspace logical server.

To add a server component:

1 From the navigation tree, select the SAS server and select **Add Application Server Component** from the pop-up menu, the **Actions** menu, or the toolbar. The New Server Component Wizard starts.

2 Use the SAS Server Type window to specify what kind of SAS server you want to add to the server.

Display 5.10 New Server Component Wizard – SAS Server Type Window

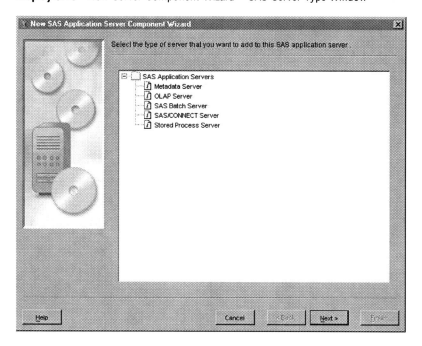

The server types available are those that are not already present in the server. In this example, the server already contained a workspace server, so that type is not listed. Select the server type and click Next to continue.

3 The SAS Server Configuration window lets you choose the type of client connection for the server.

Display 5.11 New Server Component Wizard – SAS Server Configuration Window

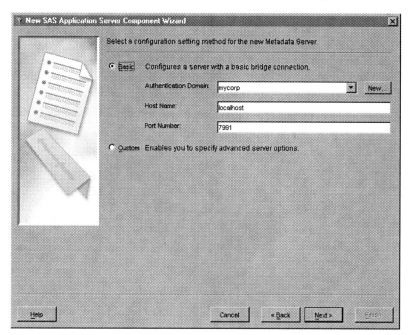

Select **Basic** to define an IOM Bridge connection using default values for all options not listed on this window. Select **Custom** to define an IOM Bridge

connection that does not use default values or to define a COM connection. For this example, we will select **Basic**.

4 The Finish window lists all of the information you specified in the wizard. If any of the information is incorrect, click ⟨Back⟩ to return to the appropriate window to make the correction. If all of the information is correct, click ⟨Finish⟩ to define the new server component.

5 In the navigation tree, open the SAS server to view the server component you added.

Display 5.12 Navigation Tree – SAS Server Component Added

The server contains the new logical server and corresponding physical server.

Adding a Physical Server

After logical servers are defined for a server, you can add additional physical servers to a selected logical server. Adding additional physical servers permits multiple servers of the same type to share resources and metadata definitions. Adding servers also lets you implement server pooling and load balancing. You must verify that the server type supports multiple servers in a logical server (for example, metadata and OLAP logical servers cannot contain more than one physical server).

To add a physical server:

1 Under the Server Manager in the navigation tree, open the SAS server and select the logical server to which you want to add a physical server. Select **Add Server** from the pop-up menu, the **Actions** menu, or the toolbar. The New Server Wizard starts.

2 Use the Name and Description window to provide a name for the new server definition.

Display 5.13   New Server Wizard – Name and Description Window

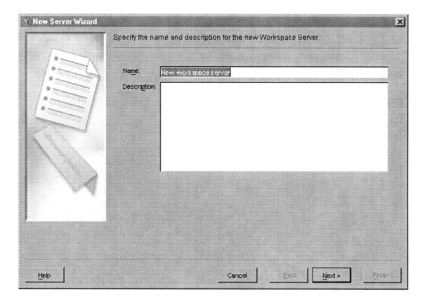

Click Next to continue.

3 Verify the server software in the Server Options window. Click Advanced Options to specify options such as file navigation options. Click Next to continue.

4 In the SAS Connection Type window, specify whether the server will use the **Bridge** protocol or the **COM** protocol to connect with clients.

5 If you selected **Bridge** as the connection protocol, use the Connection Options window to specify details about the connection. Click Next to view the Finish window.

If you specified **COM** as the connection protocol, use the COM Connection Options window to specify the server host name. Click Next to view the Finish window.

6 Use the Finish window to review the information you specified in the wizard. If you need to make changes, click Back to return to the appropriate window. If the information is correct, click Finish to create the server definition.

7 The new server is visible under the appropriate logical server in the navigation tree.

Display 5.14   Navigation Tree – Physical Server Added

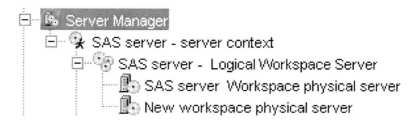

Adding a Server Connection

If a server supports both COM and IOM Bridge protocols for connections between the server and clients, you can define a second connection method for a server. For example, if you initially defined the server to use an IOM Bridge connection, you can also define a COM connection.

To define a new connection for a server:

1 From the navigation tree, select the server for which you want to define a connection and select **Add Connection** from the pop-up menu, the **Actions** menu, or the toolbar. The New Connection Wizard starts.

2 The SAS Connection Type window lets you specify the connection to add to the server.

Display 5.15 New Connection Wizard – SAS Connection Type Window

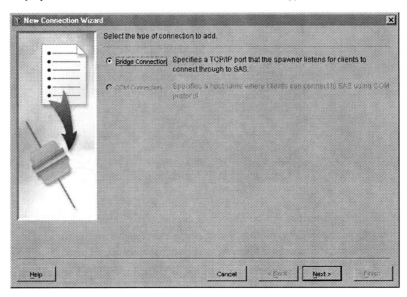

If a connection type has already been defined for the server, that type is unavailable in this window. Select the connection type and click Next to continue.

3 Complete the wizard for the connection type you selected.

4 When the definition is complete, select the server in the navigation tree to view the defined server connections in the display area.

Display 5.16 New Connections List

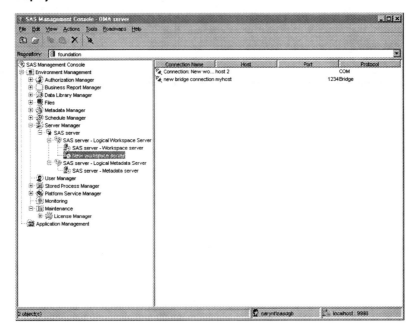

Defining a SAS Spawner

If you are defining a SAS server that uses IOM Bridge protocol for connections to remote clients, you must use a spawner to set up connections between the server and clients. A spawner is a type of SAS server that runs on a remote machine and listens for requests from clients who want to use a server.

Figure 5.2   Object Spawner Operation

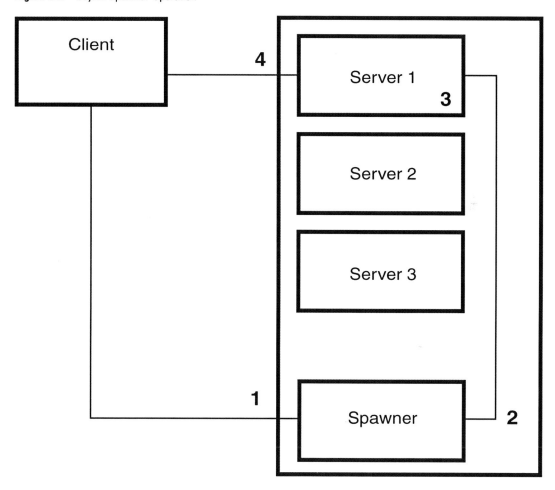

The spawner operates using this procedure:

1 The spawner receives a request for a SAS server session on the spawner's listening port.

2 The spawner passes the request to a server.

3 The server starts a SAS session.

4 The server responds to the client, and all further communications are between the client and server.

By using a spawner, you can define multiple servers on a single machine and have all requests from clients sent to the same port (the spawner listening port).

To set up a spawner environment:

1 Plan the object spawner environment by determining this information:

□ the machine on which the servers and spawners run

□ the port that the spawner will use to listen for requests from clients

□ the login ID that will be used to start the spawner session

□ the login ID that will be used to log on to the spawner machine to perform queries and maintenance

□ the relevant information (such as name, port number, and type) for the servers that will be started by the spawner.

2 Use the User Manager plug-in to define the login IDs for starting the spawner and for logging on to the spawner to perform maintenance. Define the IDs as new users, and specify the machine on which the spawner runs as the domain value for the users. See "Defining a User" on page 46 for details about defining a new user.

3 Use the Server Manager plug-in to define the SAS servers that will be started by the object spawner. This step is optional at this point, because you can also define the SAS servers during the process of defining the spawner.

4 Select the Server Manager plug-in, and select **New Server** from the pop-up menu, the **Actions** menu, or the toolbar.

5 In the Server Type window, locate the SAS Servers folder and the Spawners subfolder, then select **Object Spawner** as the server type.

Display 5.17 New Server Wizard – Object Spawner Selected

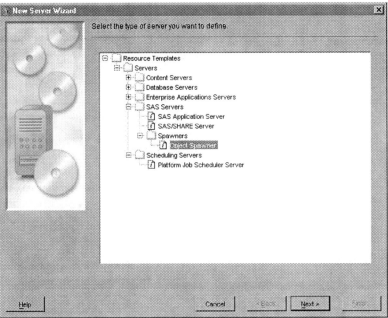

Click Next to continue.

6 In the Name and Description window, provide a name for the spawner and click Next.

7 In the Server Options window, verify the software details and specify the listed details.

Display 5.18 New Server Wizard – Server Options Window

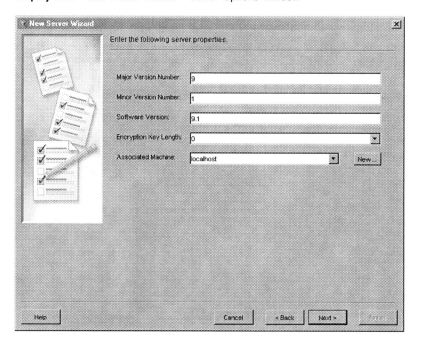

In the **Associated Machine** field, specify the machine on which the spawner runs. The spawner must run on the same machine as the servers that the spawner will be starting. Click ‾Next‾ to continue.

8 In the Spawner Initialization window, select a login that will be used to start the spawner session.

Display 5.19 New Server Wizard – Spawner Initialization Window

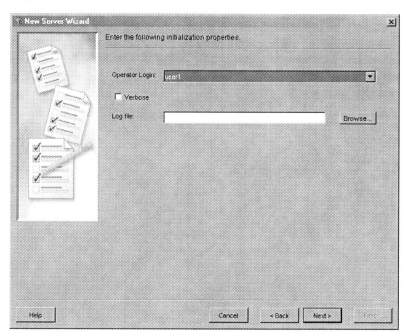

Select a login ID that has been defined for the spawner's domain from the **Operator Login** drop-down list. See "Defining a User" on page 46 for information

about defining a login ID. Specify the path and name of the spawner log file and select the **Verbose** check box if you want the file to include detailed messages. Click $\boxed{\text{Next}}$ to continue.

9 In the Spawned Servers window, choose the SAS servers that the spawner should start.

Display 5.20   New Server Wizard – Spawned Servers Window

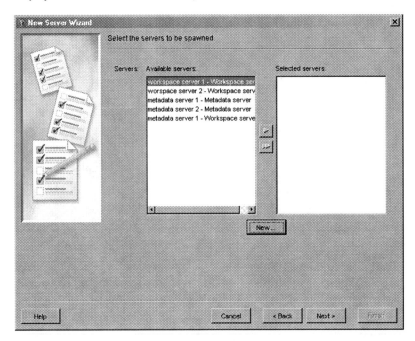

The window lists all servers that have been defined to run on the machine specified in the **Associated Machine** field on the Server Options window. Because a server can only be associated with a single spawner, only servers that have not already been associated with a spawner are listed. If no servers are listed, click $\boxed{\text{New}}$ to start the New Server Wizard and define a new server. Click $\boxed{\text{Next}}$ to continue.

10 The Spawner Connection Type window lets you specify the special-use connections for the spawner.

Display 5.21 New Server Wizard – Spawner Connection Type Window

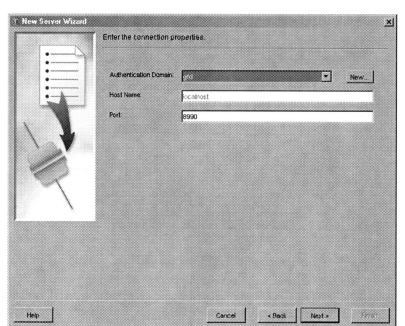

Because an operator connection to the spawner is required, the **Operator Connection** radio button is the only option available when first defining the spawner. An administrator uses an operator connection to log on to the spawner to perform maintenance or queries. After you have defined the spawner, you can use the **Add Connection** option to add a UUID connection or a load-balance connection. Click ⌴Next⌴ to continue.

11 In the Connection Options window, specify the details for the operator connection to the spawner.

Display 5.22 New Server Wizard – Connection Options Window

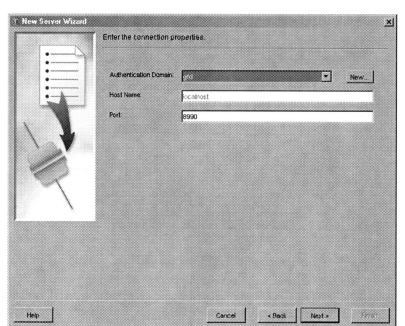

The value for the **Host Name** field is set to the host for the spawner, and cannot be changed. In the **Port** field, specify the port that the operator or administrator will use to log on to the spawner machine to perform maintenance. Click Next to continue.

12 The Finish window lists all of the information you specified in the wizard. Click Back to correct any incorrect information; otherwise, click Finish to define the spawner.

Setting Up Load Balancing

Load balancing spreads out client requests across several server processes, with new servers being automatically started based on demand. You can only use load balancing with IOM Bridge connections, not COM connections. Load balancing is most useful for applications that require a server for a short period of time. For detailed information about load balancing, see *SAS Intelligence Platform: Application Server Administration Guide*.

To implement load balancing, you must convert a logical server to a load-balanced server, then set up the individual servers for load balancing. You can convert workspace or stored process logical servers to load-balanced servers. You must also define an object spawner to start the load-balancing servers, and define a load-balancing connection for the spawner.

To implement load balancing:

1 Use the User Manager plug-in to define a login that will be used for spawner-to-spawner connections.

2 In the Server Manager plug-in, open a server and select the logical server you want to convert to a load-balanced server. Select**Convert To ▶ Load Balancing** from the pop-up menu or the **Actions** menu. A message appears asking you to confirm that you want to convert the server. Click OK to continue.

3 Use the Load Balancing Options window to set up the load balancing parameters.

Display 5.23 Load Balancing Options Window

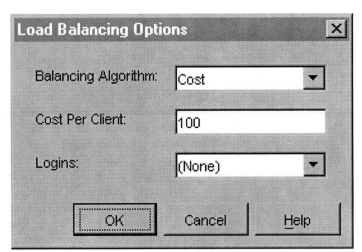

Currently, cost is the only available balancing algorithm. In the **Cost Per Client** field, specify the weight that each client connection carries. The cost is added to the total cost of the server when the client connects, and subtracted when the client disconnects. In the **Logins** field, specify a login to use for spawner-to spawner connections. Click OK to convert the logical server to a load-balancing server. If you select the server in the navigation tree, the entry in the display area indicates that the logical server is now a load-balanced server.

Display 5.24 Load-Balancing Server Designation

Name	Description	Role
SAS server - Logical Workspa...		Load Balancing
SAS server - Logical Metadata...		Standard

4 Next, you must set up the load-balancing parameters for each server in the logical server. You cannot set up load balancing for a server that uses COM for client connections. Select a server under the load-balancing logical server and select **Properties** from the pop-up menu or the **File** menu. In the Properties window, select the Options tab and then click Advanced Options .

5 In the Advanced Options window, select the Load Balancing Properties tab.

6 Use the Load Balancing Properties tab to specify load balancing parameters for an individual server.

Display 5.25 Load Balancing Properties Tab

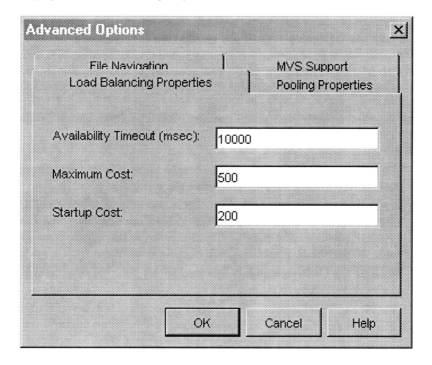

Enter information for the following:

Availability Timeout specifies the number of milliseconds to wait for a server to become available. This value is used when all servers are connected to the maximum allowed number of clients.

Maximum Cost specifies the maximum cost allowed on the server before requests to the server are denied. Use the value for the **Cost Per Client** field (from the Load Balancing Options window) to determine this value based on the number of client connections allowed.

Startup Cost   specifies the startup cost for the server. If the startup cost is less than the cost per client, each client will connect to a different server. If the startup cost is greater than or equal to the maximum cost, client connections first go to the same server.

Click $\boxed{\text{OK}}$ in the open windows for the server. When you close the Properties window, the load-balancing options are applied to the server.

7 Set load-balancing options for each server under the logical server.

8 From the Server Manager plug-in, start the New Server Wizard to create an object spawner definition. Select the servers that are participating in load balancing as the servers that the spawner should start. See "Defining a SAS Spawner" on page 71 for details about defining a spawner.

9 After the spawner definition is complete, add a load balance connection to the spawner definition. See "Adding a Server Connection" on page 69 for details about adding a connection.

Setting Up Pooling

Pooling lets you set up a pool of connections to a group of servers. When a client requests a server connection, the connection is allocated from the pool, then released back to the pool when no longer needed. Without pooling, client connections remain active and use resources even if the connection is not active.

The connection pool consists of one or more puddles, each of which connects to a server using a specified user name and password. You can use puddles to enable connections over multiple domains or to customize server permissions for specific user classes.

For detailed information about pooling, see *SAS Intelligence Platform: Application Server Administration Guide*.

To set up pooling:

1 Use the User Manager plug-in to create login IDs to access each puddle in the pool. Every puddle must have a unique login ID.

2 In the Server Manager plug-in, open a server and select the logical server you want to convert to a pooling server. Select**Convert To ▶ Pooling** from the pop-up menu or the **Actions** menu. A message appears asking you to confirm that you want to convert the server. Click $\boxed{\text{OK}}$ to continue.

3 The Pooling Options window lets you select the puddles that should be in the pool.

Display 5.26 Pooling Options Window

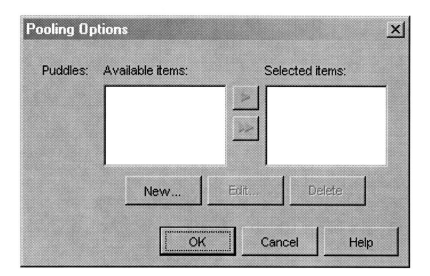

If you are setting up pooling for the first time, no puddles are listed in the **Available items** list. Click New to define a new puddle.

4 Use the New Puddle window to define the puddle parameters.

Display 5.27 New Puddle Window

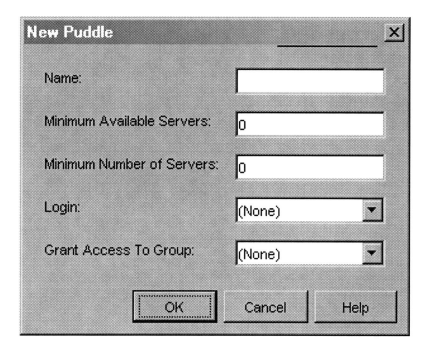

Specify the following information:

Name	specifies the name of the puddle.
Minimum Available Servers	specifies the minimum number of idle server connections that should always be available.

Minimum Number of Servers	specifies the minimum number of server connections that are created when the pool is created. This value includes both connections that are in use and ones that are idle.
Login	specifies the user login for the pool.
Grant Access To Group	specifies the user group that can access the puddle.

Click OK in the New Puddle window, then click OK in the Pooling Options window to convert the server to a pooling server

5 Next, you must set up the pooling parameters for each server in the logical server. Select a server under the pooling logical server and select **Properties** from the pop-up menu or the **File** menu. In the Properties window, select the Options tab and then click Advanced Options .

6 In the Advanced Options window, select the Pooling Properties tab to specify the pooling parameters for the server.

Display 5.28   Pooling Properties Tab

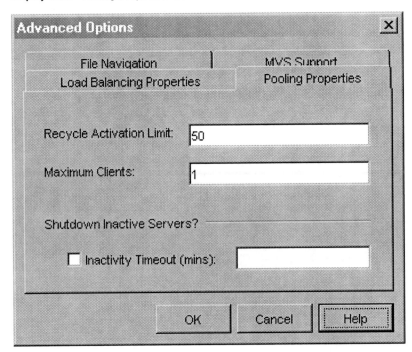

Specify the following parameters:

Recycle Activation Limit	specifies the number of times a connection to the server is reused before it is disconnected. If you specify a value of 0, there is no limit to the number of times the connection can be reused.
Maximum Clients	specifies the maximum number of SAS workspaces you want to allocate to each pool. When specifying this value, you should consider the number and type of processors on the server machine, the amount of memory on the machine, the type of clients that will be making requests, and the number of different pools in which the server participates.
Inactivity Timeout	specifies whether an idle server should remain running or should shut down after a specified time. If you do not select the

check box, then idle servers remain running. If you select the check box, servers run for the number of minutes you specify in the **Inactivity Timeout** field.

Click OK in the open windows for the server. When you close the Properties window, the pooling options are applied to the server.

7 Repeat these steps to set up pooling options for each server under the logical server.

Managing Database Servers

A database server is a machine that contains data from a program other than SAS. You can use SAS Management Console to create definitions for database servers containing data from many different applications, enabling other applications to access the data.

Because each type of application data is accessed differently, the process of defining a database server is slightly different for each type of database server. However, the basic information that is required is the same for all database server types:

□ server name

□ machine on which the server runs

□ location of the data

□ credentials for logging on to the server

To define a database server:

1 From the navigation tree, select the Server Manager plug-in and then select **New Server** from the pop-up menu, toolbar, or **Actions** menu. The New Server Wizard starts.

2 Use the Server Type window to select the server you are defining.

Display 5.29   New Server Wizard – Selecting a Database Server Type

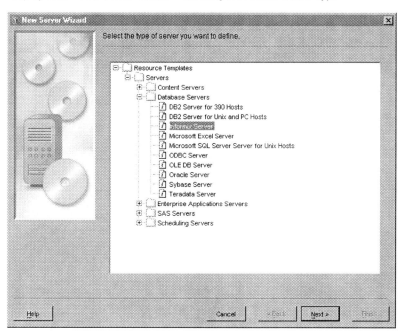

Locate the Database Servers folder and select the server for the type of data you want to access. For this example, select **Informix Server** and click Next to continue.

3 In the Name and Description window, specify a name and (optionally) a description for the server. Click Next to continue.

4 In the Server Options window, verify that the server software information is correct and select the machine on which the server runs.

Display 5.30   New Server Wizard – Server Options Window

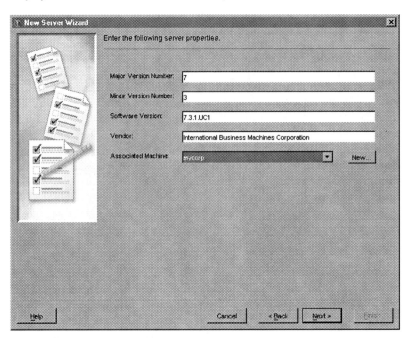

If the machine is not included in the **Associated Machine** drop-down list, click New to specify a new machine name.

If you are defining an OLE/DB or ODBC database server, you must also specify the type of OLE/DB or ODBC data contained on the server. Refer to the Help for the Server Options window for details.

Click Next to continue.

5 In the Connection Options window, specify the location of the data on the server and the information needed to access the data.

Display 5.31 New Server Wizard – Connection Options for Informix Server

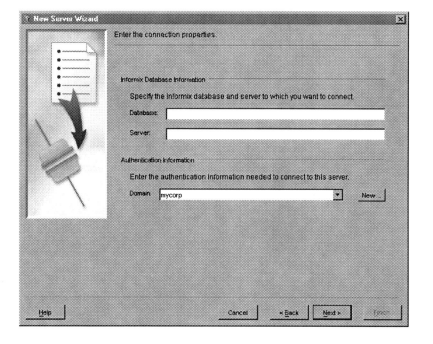

For this example, you must specify the Informix database you want to access and the Informix server on which the database resides. You must also specify the domain that will be used to authenticate login attempts to the server.

The connection properties are different for each type of database server. Click Help for detailed information about the fields for the specific type of server you are defining. Click Next to continue.

6 The Finish window lists all of the information you specified in the wizard. Click Back to correct any incorrect information; otherwise click Finish to define the database server.

Managing Enterprise Application Servers

An enterprise application server is a machine that is used to run a data analysis or access application other than SAS. Enterprise application servers let SAS applications such as SAS Data Integration Studio and SAS Data Surveyors navigate and locate information in applications such as SAP, Siebel, Oracle Applications, and PeopleSoft.

As with database servers, the definition process for each enterprise application server is different. In general, you must name the server and identify a database server for the enterprise application.

To define an enterprise application server:

1 From the navigation tree, select the Server Manager plug-in and then select **New Server** from the pop-up menu, toolbar, or **Actions** menu. The New Server Wizard starts.

2 Use the Server Type window to select the server you are defining.

Display 5.32 New Server Wizard – Selecting an Enterprise Application Server

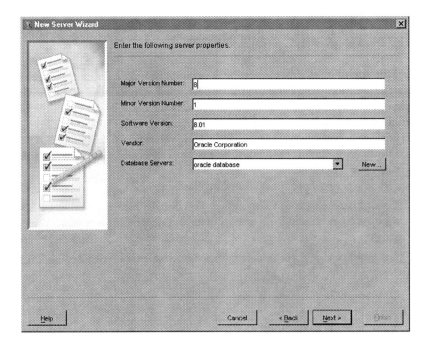

Locate the Enterprise Applications Servers folder and select the server for the type
of data you want to access. Click Next to continue.

3 In the Name and Description window, specify a name and (optionally) a
description for the server. Click Next to continue.

4 In the Server Options window, verify that the server software information is
correct and select the database server for the enterprise application.

Display 5.33 New Server Wizard – Server Options Window

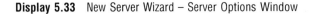

If the server you want to use is not listed in the **Database Servers** drop-down list, click New to start a new instance of the New Server Wizard to define a new database server. See "Managing Database Servers" on page 81 for information about defining a database server.

If you are defining an SAP application server, you do not need to specify a database server.

Click Next to continue. For Oracle Applications, Siebel, and PeopleSoft application servers, clicking Next takes you to the Finish window.

5 If you are defining an SAP application server, you must specify how clients will connect to the SAP server.

Display 5.34 New Server wizard – SAP Connection Options Window

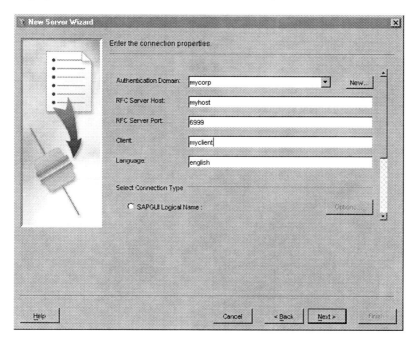

In addition to specifying the connection information, such as authentication domain, RFC server host, and RFC server port, you must also select a connection type. Scroll to the bottom of the window and select one of the connection types listed, then click Options for the selected type and specify the required information. Click Help for detailed information about the options in this window.

Click Next to continue.

6 The Finish window lists all of the information you specified in the wizard. Click Back to correct any incorrect information; otherwise click Finish to define the application server.

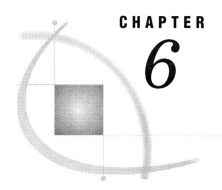

Managing Libraries

What Is the Data Library Manager?

The Data Library Manager is a SAS Management Console plug-in used to create metadata definitions for data libraries and database schemas. The definitions are stored in the SAS Metadata Repository and are then available for other applications to use. You can use the plug-in to manage SAS data libraries, libraries containing data from other applications, and libraries used directly by other applications. You can also create definitions for database schemas, which are existing maps of the data structure of a database.

The plug-in provides support for a wide variety of library types through the use of resource templates. A resource template is an XML file that specifies the information required to define a certain type of resource (such as a library). See "Managing Resource Templates" on page 38 for more information about resource templates. Many of the library types available correspond to the engine types specified on the SAS LIBNAME statement, with the options available for the library definition corresponding to the LIBNAME options for the engine. In addition, library types are available for a generic library (a definition without an engine name already supplied) and a pre-assigned library (a definition for a library assigned by SAS during initialization, such as SASUSER or WORK).

The information specified for each library definition corresponds to options on the LIBNAME statement. Refer to the Help for each window in the Data Library Manager for information about the correlation between fields in the plug-in and LIBNAME options.

Before you can begin creating definitions in the Data Library Manager plug-in, you must perform these tasks:

- [ ] For SAS libraries, determine the libref and path for the SAS library and, optionally, decide to which SAS servers the library will be assigned.

□ For database libraries, define a database server and database schema of the same type as the database library. You can also define these from within the New Library wizard.

□ For database schemas, define a database server and determine the name of the existing data schema. You can also define the server from within the New Library Wizard.

Defining SAS Libraries

The Data Library Manager provides resource templates for several types of SAS libraries. The procedure for defining and editing each of these libraries (except for SAS/SHARE libraries) is identical. However, the Advanced Options window contains fields that are specific to each library type. See "Managing SAS/SHARE Remote Engine Libraries" on page 91 for specific information about SAS/SHARE libraries.

To define a SAS library:

1 From the navigation tree, open the Library Manager plug-in and then select the SAS Libraries folder. Select **New Library** from the pop-up menu, the toolbar, or the **Actions** menu. The New Library Wizard starts.

2 Use the Library Type window to select the type of library you are defining.

Display 6.1   New Library Wizard – Library Type Window

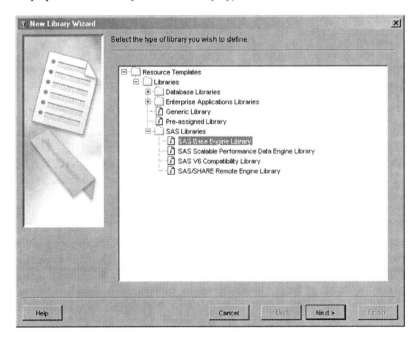

Open the SAS Libraries folder and select a SAS library type. This example uses the **SAS Base Engine Library**. Click ⎡Next⎤ to continue.

3 In the Name window, specify a name for the library definition and a description (optional). The name you specify in this window is the name that will be used to identify the definition in SAS Management Console; it is not the LIBREF library name as specified on a LIBNAME statement.

Display 6.2 New Library Wizard – Name Window

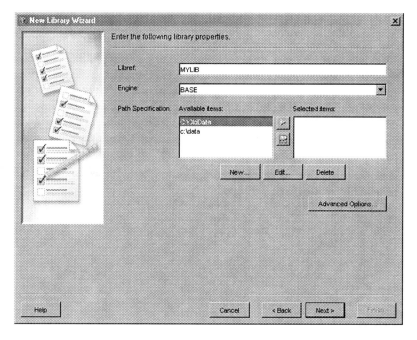

Click [Next] to continue.

4 Use the Library Options window to specify the SAS libref, engine, and path for the library.

Display 6.3 New Library Wizard – Library Options Window

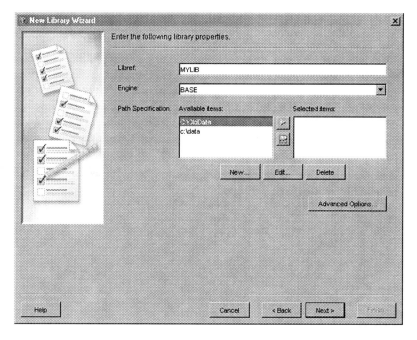

The `Path Specification` field specifies the path for the library on the server. Any paths that have already been specified for libraries are listed in the `Available items` list. Use the arrow controls to move a path from the `Available items` list to the `Selected items` list. You can also click [New] to display the New

Path Specification window in order to specify a path. Note that the Browse button on the New Path Specification window can only be used to select a directory on the local machine, not on the server.

5 Click Advanced Options to display the Advanced Options window.

Display 6.4   New Library Wizard – Advanced Options Window

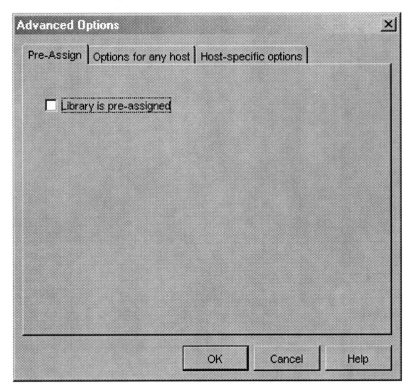

This window lets you pre-assign a library, specify library options for any host, and specify host-specific options. See "Managing Pre-Assigned Libraries" on page 100 for information about pre-assigned libraries. All options on this window correspond to SAS LIBNAME options. The tabs and fields in this window are different for each type of SAS library. For information about a specific option, click Help from any tab. Click OK to close the Advanced Options window and return to the Library Options window. Click Next to continue.

6 Use the SAS Server window to optionally specify the SAS servers that will have access to the library.

Display 6.5 New Library Wizard – SAS Server Window

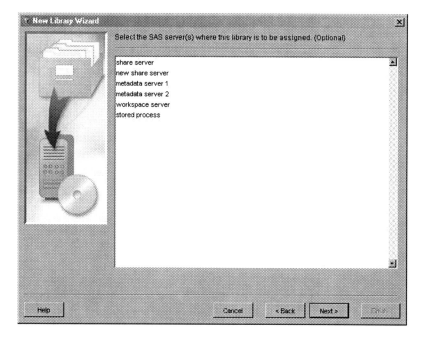

This window lists all of the SAS servers that have already been defined using the Server Manager plug-in. Select all of the servers for which this library should be assigned. Click ⟨Next⟩ to continue.

7 The Finish window lists all of the information you specified in the wizard. If you need to make any corrections, click ⟨Back⟩ to return to the appropriate window. If all the information is correct. click ⟨Finish⟩ to define the library.

Managing SAS/SHARE Remote Engine Libraries

The SAS/SHARE remote engine library creates a library reference to a SAS/SHARE server and a library that has already been defined on the server. Using the SAS/ SHARE Remote Library Services (RLS) capability, you can define a shared connection to a permanent SAS data library.

1 Verify that a server definition has been created for the SAS/SHARE server. See "Defining a Basic SAS Server" on page 61 for information about defining a server.

2 Using the Data Library Manager, first create a **SAS Base Engine Library** definition for the shared SAS library that you want to access using Remote Library Services. You must assign the library to the SAS/SHARE server.

Display 6.6   Assign a Library to a SAS/SHARE Server

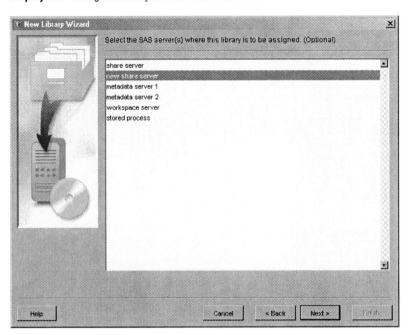

3 After creating the shared SAS library, use the Data Library Manager to create a definition for a **SAS/SHARE Remote Engine Library**. After you select the library type, use the wizard to specify the definition name, libref, and advanced options (if necessary).

4 Use the SAS/SHARE Server window to specify the SAS/SHARE server and shared library to which the remote engine library should point.

Display 6.7   New Server Wizard – SAS/SHARE Server Window

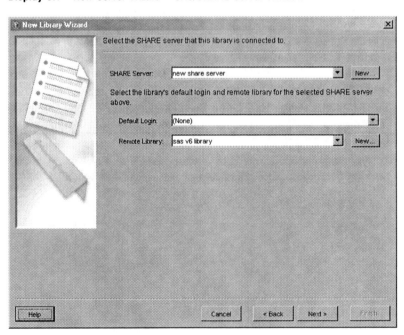

Select the server you defined in step 1 from the **SHARE Server** drop-down list. If you did not previously define a server, you can click New to start the New Server Wizard, which you can use to define a SAS/SHARE server.

After you select the server, select the shared library you defined in step 2 from the **Remote Library** drop-down list. The library you select is the library that the remote engine library will access. If you have not defined a library, you can click New to start another instance of the New Library Wizard, which you can use to define the shared SAS library.

Specify the default ID that will be used to make connections to the SAS/SHARE server. Click Next to continue with the rest of the New Library Wizard and define the library.

Managing Database Schemas

A database schema definition is a pointer to an already-existing schema, which is a map or model of the structure of a database. You must create a definition for a type of database schema before you can define a database library of that same type. For example, you must create a definition for an ODBC schema before you can define an ODBC database library.

To define a database schema:

1 Use the Server Manager plug-in to create a database server definition that matches the type of schema you want to define. For example, you must define a Teradata database server before you can define a Teradata schema. See "Managing Database Servers" on page 81 for information about defining a database server.

2 From the navigation tree, select the Data Library Manager plug-in and then select the Database Schemas folder. Select **New Database Schema** from the pop-up menu, the **Actions** menu, or the toolbar. The New Database Schema Wizard starts.

3 Use the Type window to select the type of schema you want to define.

Display 6.8 New Database Schema Wizard – Type Window

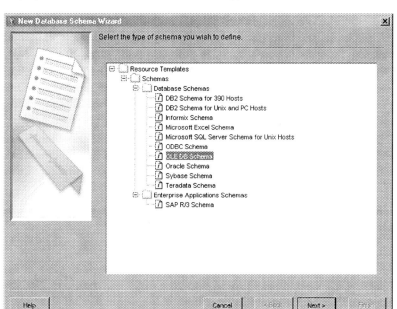

Open the Database Schemas folder and select a schema type from those listed. If the schema type you want to define is not listed, make sure the schema's resource template has been loaded. See "Managing Resource Templates" on page 38 for more information. Click Next to continue.

4 In the Name window, specify a name and description for the schema. The name you specify in this window is the name that will be used to identify the definition in SAS Management Console; it is not the schema name as specified on a LIBNAME statement. Click Next to continue.

5 In the Database Schema Options window, specify the schema name and the server for which the schema is valid.

Display 6.9   New Database Schema Wizard – Database Schema Options Window

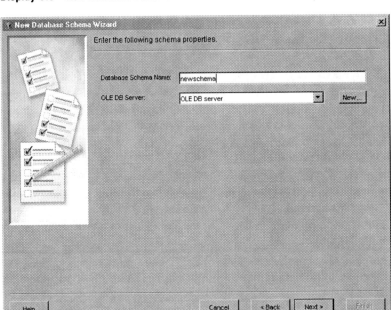

The name specified on this window is the name as specified on the LIBNAME statement.

Select a database server from the **Server** drop-down list. Only server types that match the schema type you are defining are listed. For example, if you are defining an OLE DB schema, only OLE DB database servers are listed. If the server you need is not listed, click New to start the New Server Wizard and define a database server. See "Managing Database Servers" on page 81 for more information about defining a server. Click Next to continue.

6 The Finish window contains a summary of the information you specified in the wizard. If you need to make any changes, click Back to return to the appropriate window. If everything is correct, click Finish to define the schema.

Managing Database Libraries

The Data Library Manager plug-in allows you to define SAS libraries that point to data from other databases or data analysis applications. The library definitions that you create perform the same function as a SAS/ACCESS LIBNAME statement in SAS. The information you enter in the New Library Wizard for a database library correlates to SAS/ACCESS LIBNAME options. Click Help from any window in the New Library Wizard or the library properties window for more information.

To create a database library:

1 Use the Server Manager plug-in to create a server definition for the database server. The database server is the server that contains the data you want to access. For information about creating a server definition, see "Managing Database Servers" on page 81.

2 Use the Data Library Manager to create a schema definition that specifies the model of the database for which you are creating a library definition. For example, if you are creating a Teradata library definition, you must create a definition for the schema of the Teradata database.

3 From the navigation tree, select the Data Library Manager plug-in and then select the SAS Libraries folder. Select **New Library** from the pop-up menu, the **Actions** menu, or the toolbar. The New Library Wizard starts.

4 Use the Library Type window to select the type of database library you want to define.

Display 6.10 New Library Wizard – Library Type Window

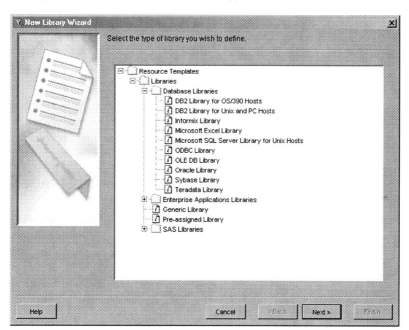

Open the Database Libraries folder or the Enterprise Applications Libraries folder and select a library type from those listed. If the library type you want to define is not listed, make sure the library's resource template has been loaded. See "Managing Resource Templates" on page 38 for more information. Click Next to continue.

5 In the Name window, specify a name and description for the library definition. The name you specify in this window is the name that will be used to identify the definition in SAS Management Console; it is not the libref as specified on a LIBNAME statement. Click Next to continue.

6 In the Library Options window, specify the libref for the database library.

Display 6.11 New Library Wizard – Library Options Window

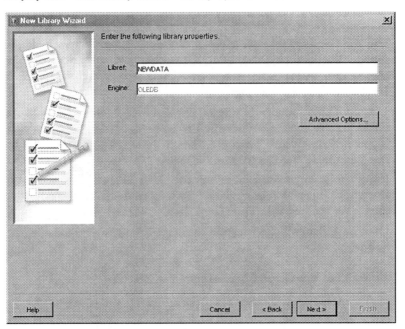

The **Engine** field already contains the correct library engine type, based on the library type you selected.

Click Advanced Options to specify the remainder of the options for the database library.

Display 6.12 New Library Wizard – Database Library Advanced Options Window

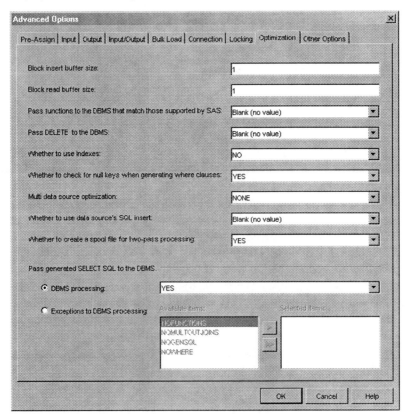

The tabs in this window and the fields displayed on each tab differ according to the type of library you are defining. The options in the Advanced Options window all correspond to options on the SAS/ACCESS LIBNAME statement for the type of library you are defining. Click [Help] on any tab for detailed information about the options on the tab. Click [OK] to close the Advanced Options window and return to the New Library Wizard. Click [Next] to continue.

7 The Database Server window lets you specify the server that contains the library's data.

Display 6.13 New Library Wizard – Database Server Window

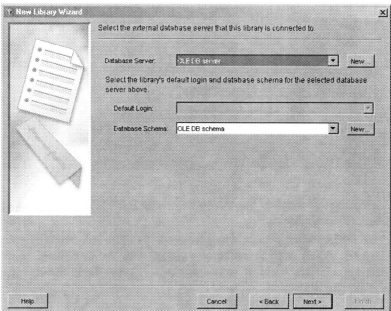

Select a defined server that matches the library type from the **Database Server** drop-down list. For example, if you are defining an OLE DB library, the **Database Server** field lists the OLE DB servers that you have defined. If the server you need is not listed, click [New] to start the New Server Wizard and create the server definition.

Select a defined schema that matches the library type from the **Database Schema** drop-down list. If you have not defined a schema, click [New] to start the New Database Schema wizard for the appropriate schema type. See "Managing Database Schemas" on page 93 for more information.

Click [Next] to continue.

8 The SAS Server window lets you specify which SAS servers will have access to the database library.

Display 6.14   New Server Wizard – SAS Server Window

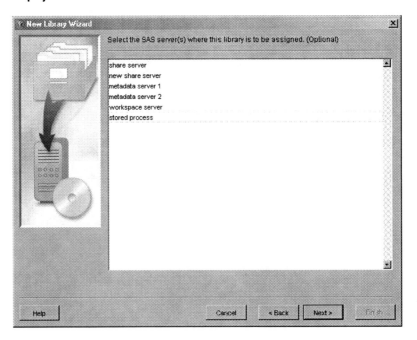

Select one or more of the defined servers from the list. This step is optional. Click [Next] to continue.

9 The Finish window contains a summary of the information you specified in the wizard. If you need to make any changes to the definition, click [Back] to return to the appropriate window in the wizard. If everything is correct, click [Finish] to define the library.

Managing Generic Libraries

The generic library type lets you manually define a library. When you select any other library type, the Data Library Manager automatically sets the library engine and the library options to those valid for the chosen type. When you select the Generic Library type, the plug-in does not set the engine and does not display a list of valid options. Using the generic library lets you create a library definition using an engine for which there is not a library type and lets you specify LIBNAME options that are not included in the existing library types. The generic library is also useful if you are an experienced user who wants to quickly define libraries based on your knowledge of the LIBNAME statement.

To define a generic library:

1 From the Data Library Manager plug-in, select the SAS Libraries folder and select **New Library** from the pop-up menu, the **Actions** menu, or the toolbar. The New Library Wizard starts.

2 In the Library Type window, select **Generic Library** as the library type.

Display 6.15 New Library Wizard – Generic Library Selected

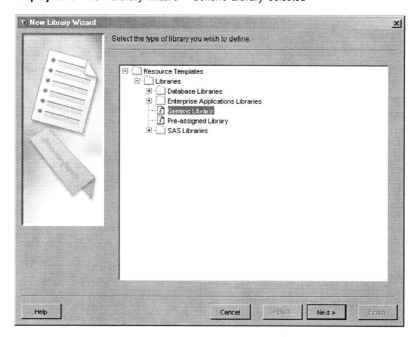

Click Next to continue.

3 In the Name window, specify a name and description for the library definition. The name you specify in this window is the name that will be used to identify the definition in SAS Management Console; it is not the libref as specified on a LIBNAME statement. Click Next to continue.

4 The Library Options window provides the basic fields you need to define a library.

Display 6.16 New Library Wizard – Library Options Window for Generic Library

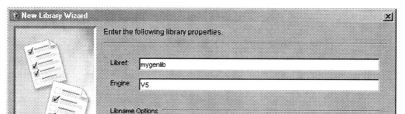

You must specify the libref and a valid LIBNAME engine for the library. You can specify any valid LIBNAME options in the **Options** field. Because the wizard does

not perform any error checking on the field, you must ensure that the options are specified correctly and that they are valid for the engine you specified.

Click Advanced Options to display the Advanced Options window, which you can use to pre-assign the library. Click Next to continue.

5 The SAS Server window lets you specify which SAS servers will have access to the library.

Display 6.17   New Library Wizard – SAS Server Window

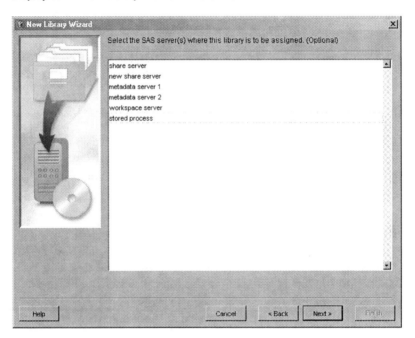

Select one or more of the defined servers from the list. This step is optional. Click Next to continue.

6 The Finish window contains a summary of the information you specified in the wizard. If you need to make any changes to the definition, click Back to return to the appropriate window in the wizard. If everything is correct, click Finish to define the library.

Managing Pre-Assigned Libraries

The Data Library Manager plug-in allows you to define two types of pre-assigned libraries:

□ a library definition that is automatically assigned whenever the server to which it is assigned is started

□ a library definition that refers to a library that is pre-assigned by SAS (such as SASUSER, SASHELP, or WORK)

To specify a library as pre-assigned for a server, select the **Library is Pre-Assigned** check box in the library's Advanced Options window. This window is accessible from the Library Options window of the New Library Wizard or from the Options tab of the Properties window (for an already-defined library). After you specify that the library is preassigned, ensure that the library is assigned to the correct SAS

servers. The selected library will be assigned whenever one of the selected servers
starts.

To create a library definition for a SAS pre-assigned library:

1 Start the New Library Wizard and select **Pre-assigned Library** from the
Library Type window.

Display 6.18   New Library Wizard – Pre-Assigned Library Selected

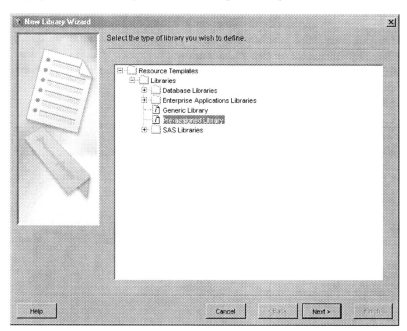

2 In the Library Options window, specify the LIBREF of a SAS pre-assigned library
(such as SASUSER, SASHELP, or WORK) in the **Libref** field. The pre-assigned
check box is automatically selected and cannot be changed.

Display 6.19   New Library Wizard – Library Options Window for Pre-Assigned Library

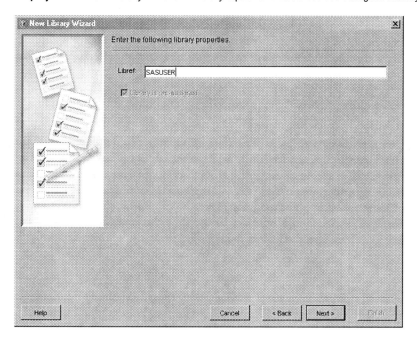

3 Finish the library definition by optionally assigning the library to one or more SAS servers and verifying all of the definition information.

Editing a Library Definition

After you have defined a SAS library, you can modify any of the properties specified when the library was defined. To view a library's properties, open the SAS Libraries folder under the Data Library Manager plug-in, select a library, and select **Properties** from the pop-up menu or the **File** menu.

The Properties window contains all of the fields displayed in the New Library Wizard.

Display 6.20 Library Properties Window

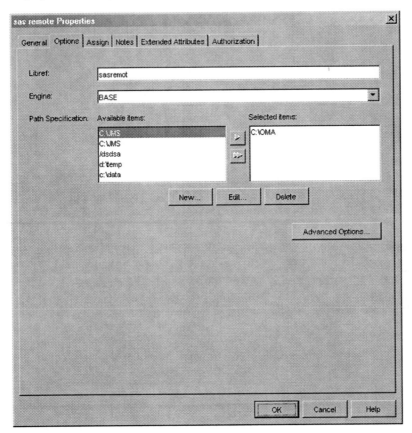

You can also assign roles for the definition, associate notes and documents, apply extended attributes, and specify authorization permissions for the definition.

If you only want to change the SAS servers to which the library is assigned, you can select the library under the SAS Libraries folder and select **Edit Assignments** from the pop-up menu or the **Actions** menu.

The Edit Assignments window lists all of the defined SAS servers and highlights the servers to which the library is assigned.

Display 6.21 Edit Assignments Window

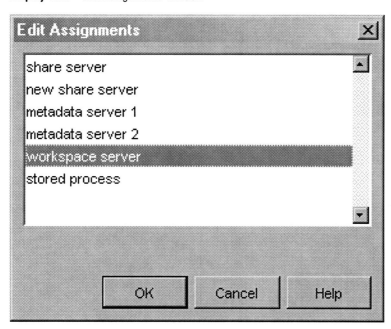

To add an assignment without removing any current assignments, press the CTRL or SHIFT keys while selecting the additional servers.

Reviewing the LIBNAME Statement

To review the generated LIBNAME statement for a SAS library definition, open the SAS Libraries folder under the Data Library Manager plug-in, select the library, and select **Display Libname** from the pop-up menu or the actions menu.

Display 6.22 Display Libname Window

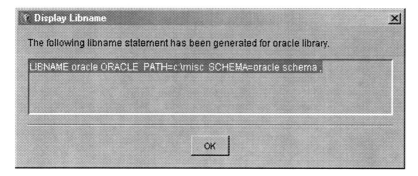

The Display Libname window lists the SAS LIBNAME statement that is generated based on the information specified when you created the library definition. This statement contains all of the options specified directly when the library definition was created. If an option was not changed from the default, that option does not appear in the generated LIBNAME statement.

You cannot change the LIBNAME statement directly from this window. You must change the library definition by using the Properties window to change the generated LIBNAME statement.

Editing a Schema Definition

After you have created a schema definition, you can modify any of the properties specified when the schema was defined. To view a schema's properties, open the Database Schemas folder under the Data Library Manager plug-in, select a schema, and select **Properties** from the pop-up menu or the **File** menu.

The Properties window contains all of the fields displayed in the New Database Schema Wizard.

Display 6.23 Schema Properties Window

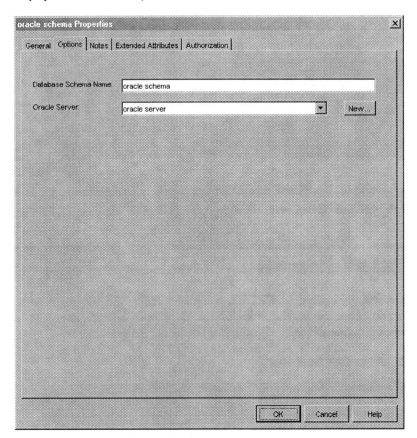

You can also assign roles for the definition, associate notes and documents, apply extended attributes, and specify authorization permissions for the schema definition.

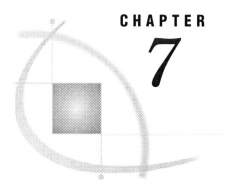

Managing Authorizations

What Is the Authorization Manager?

The Authorization Manager is a SAS Management Console plug-in that lets you create metadata definitions that control access to metadata repositories, metadata definitions within repositories, and SAS resources represented by metadata definitions. Together with the User Manager plug-in, the Authorization Manager provides an interface to the authorization facility in the SAS Metadata Server. This facility makes decisions about whether a user or group can perform a specified action on a SAS resource.

When a user tries to perform an action (such as reading or altering) on a SAS resource or its associated metadata definition, the SAS Metadata Server's authorization facility has to determine whether the user has been granted or denied permission to perform the action. The authorization facility makes this determination by using the user and group definitions created by the User Manager together with the access controls created by the Authorization Manager. The process includes checking the access controls for the resource definition as they apply to the user and any groups to which the user belongs, checking the default access permissions for the repository, and checking the access controls for all of the resource's parent definitions. See *SAS*

Intelligence Platform: Security Administration Guide for detailed information about the authorization facility.

Authorization Manager Functions

The Authorization Manager lets you

□ manage the repository access control template, which establishes the default access controls for a metadata repository

□ specify access controls for a metadata object, which define the permissions that users or groups are granted or denied for the object

□ create access control templates, which are named identity/permission patterns that can be applied to multiple metadata objects

□ manage permissions, which represent actions that users can perform on metadata objects or the computing resources represented by the objects.

Planning an Authorization Strategy

The access controls provided by the Authorization Manager are only a part of the overall security strategy necessary in a business intelligence environment. You use the Authorization Manager to implement parts of your security strategy, rather than to design a strategy. See *SAS Intelligence Platform: Security Administration Guide* for detailed information about designing and implementing a security strategy.

In general, you need to perform these tasks to implement authorization using SAS Management Console:

1 Understand the default access permissions that are provided.

2 Create definitions for users and user groups through the User Manager plug-in. Before you can define specific access controls for a user, you must establish a metadata identity for the user. See Chapter 4, "Managing Users," on page 45 for more information.

3 Configure the repository access control template (ACT), to define default access settings for all definitions in the repository.

4 Locate metadata objects to which you want to apply specialized access controls.

5 Apply access controls to individual objects.

Understanding Default Permissions

SAS Management Console manages definitions for permissions, each of which specifies a type of action that can be performed on a metadata definition or the SAS resource represented by the definitions. When you define an access control for a metadata definition or create an access control template, you specify whether a user or group is allowed or denied each of these permissions for a metadata definition.

A set of default permission definitions is automatically created when you create a foundation repository. You should understand the function of each of these permissions before you begin the process of implementing access controls. These definitions cannot be modified.

The default permissions are as follows:

Table 7.1 Metadata Permissions

Permission	Description	Enforced by
ReadMetadata	Reading a metadata definition	metadata server
WriteMetadata	Creating, updating, or deleting a metadata definition	metadata server
CheckinMetadata	Checking metadata in and out between a custom or foundation repository and a project repository	metadata server
Create	Adding data to a SAS resource described by a metadata definition	application
Delete	Deleting data from a SAS resource described by a metadata definition	application
Read	Reading data from a SAS resource described by a metadata definition	application
Write	Updating data in a SAS resource described by a metadata definition	application
Administer	Accessing administrative functions of SAS servers	application

Note: Not all applications enforce all permissions. △

You can also create and modify your own permission definitions if you are using an application that implements authorization based on the permission. See "Managing Permissions" on page 126 for information about creating and modifying permission definitions.

Locating Resources

On a SAS Metadata Server, computing resources are represented by metadata objects. Some of these objects correspond to the metadata definitions created in SAS Management Console (such as libraries and servers), some objects are created by other applications that use the metadata server (such as SAS Data Integration Studio), and some objects are created as a component of a larger metadata definition (such as the machine associated with a server). If you want to apply access controls to a metadata object, you must be able to locate the object in SAS Management Console. See "Specifying Access Controls" on page 115 for information about applying access controls to an object.

Several methods of locating objects are available, depending on the object type

SAS Management Console plug-in	enables you to locate objects created by the plug-in.
By Application	enables you to locate objects created by an application that stores metadata in the metadata repository (for example, SAS Data Integration Studio).
By Location	enables you to locate objects that are associated with a server or library definition.
By Type	enables you to locate all objects stored in the metadata repository.

Locating Resources Using Plug-ins

Metadata objects or definitions that are created by SAS Management Console plug-ins are displayed within the plug-in's navigation tree. Examples of objects that are created by plug-ins are

- □ SAS libraries and database schemas (Data Library Manager)
- □ servers and server connections (Server Manager)
- □ users and user groups (User Manager)

To display a list of metadata objects defined by a plug-in, open the plug-in in the SAS Management Console navigation tree, then select or open any appropriate sub-folders under the plug-in. If you select the folder, the objects are displayed in the display area; if you open the folder, the objects are displayed in the navigation tree.

To manage the authorization for an object, select the object in the navigation tree or display area and select **Properties** from the pop-up menu or the **File** menu. In the Properties window, select the Authorization tab. See "Specifying Access Controls" on page 115 for information about setting authorizations from the Authorization tab.

Note: Not all objects defined by plug-ins have a corresponding Properties window. △

Locating Resources by Application

Some metadata objects are defined and stored in the metadata server by applications other than SAS Management Console. You can use the Authorization Manager to locate and set the access controls for these objects. Examples of applications that store metadata objects on the metadata server are SAS Data Integration Studio, SAS XML LIBNAME Engine, and SAS Integration Technologies.

To locate resources associated with an application:

1 Verify that you are connected to the same metadata server that the application used when creating the metadata objects.

2 From the navigation tree, select the Authorization Manager plug-in and then the Resource Management folder.

3 Under the Resource Management folder, open the By Application folder.

The By Application folder contains entries for all installed applications or application groups that write metadata to the SAS Metadata Server.

Display 7.1 Resource Listing by Application

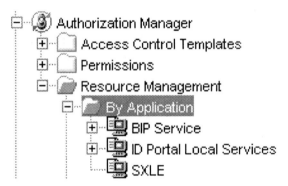

4 Click the plus sign (+) next to an application to view the subfolders and objects associated with the application.

Display 7.2 Resource Listing for ID Portal Local Services

The organization in the By Application folder reflects the object hierarchy and inheritance. Objects that are associated with an application or another object will also inherit the access controls of the parent. For example, in the preceding display, the access controls for the object "BIP Stored Process Service" by default are the same as the controls on the object "ID Portal Local Services". You can change the access controls on an object to override the defaults.

5 Select the object for which you want to set access controls and select **Properties** from the pop-up menu or the **File** menu. In the Properties window, select the Authorization tab. See "Specifying Access Controls" on page 115 for information about setting access controls using the Authorization tab.

CAUTION:
Use extreme caution when making any changes to these resources. Changing the permissions on a resource could make the resource unavailable to applications and users. △

6 After you have set the access controls, click OK to close the Properties window.

Locating Resources by Location

Some metadata objects that are created in SAS Management Console or in other applications are associated with metadata locations. These locations are metadata objects to which other objects can be associated. For example, a SAS library definition can be associated with a SAS server definition, and a database schema can be associated with a database server. Although these objects are accessible through SAS Management Console plug-ins, the By Location function assists you in locating and managing resources that have a common association.

To locate resources by location:

1 From the navigation tree, select the Authorization Manager plug-in and then the Resource Management folder.

2 Under the Resource Management folder, open the By Location folder.

3 The By Location folder contains entries for all defined metadata objects to which other objects can be associated.

Display 7.3   Resource Listing by Location

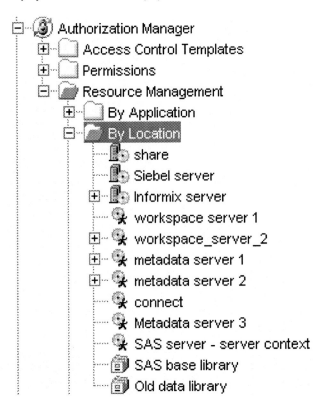

4 To view the objects associated with a location, select the location or click the plus sign (+) next to the location. The associated objects are listed in the display area (if you select the location) or the navigation tree (if you click the plus sign).

Display 7.4   Resources for a Specific Location

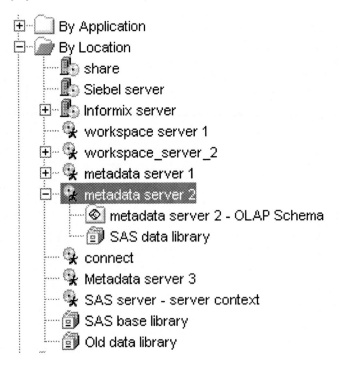

5 The organization in the By Location folder generally reflects the object hierarchy and inheritance. Objects that are associated with a location will also inherit the access controls of the location. For example, in the preceding display, the access controls for the object "SAS data library" by default are the same as the controls on the object "metadata server 2". You can change the access controls on an object to override the defaults.

6 Select an object for which you want to set access controls and select **Properties** from the pop-up menu or the **File** menu. In the Properties window, select Authorization. See "Specifying Access Controls" on page 115 for information about setting access controls using the Authorization tab.

CAUTION:
   Use extreme caution when making any changes to these resources. Changing the permissions on a resource could make the resource unavailable to applications and users. △

7 After you have set the access controls, click OK to close the Properties window.

Locating Resources by Type

To gain access to every metadata object stored on the metadata server, whether created by SAS Management Console or other applications, you must use the Authorization Manager's By Type function. This function lets you locate and view properties for every metadata object in the repository, whether it is an object that is accessible through other methods (such as a server definition) or one that is only accessible through the By Type function (such as a user login).

To locate resources by type:

1 From the navigation tree, select the Authorization Manager plug-in and then the Resource Management folder.

2 Under the Resource Management folder, open the By Type folder.

3 The By Type folder contains a folder for each type of metadata object that can be stored on the metadata server.

Display 7.5 Resources Listed by Type

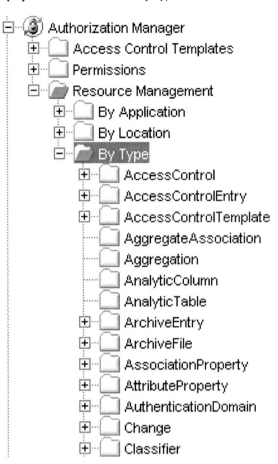

4   To view the objects of a selected type, click the plus sign (+) or select the type folder. The objects are listed in the navigation tree (if you clicked the plus sign) or the display area (if you selected the folder). Depending on the contents of the metadata server, some of the folders might not contain objects.

Display 7.6 Resources Listed for a Specific Type

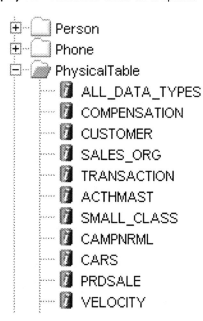

5 Select an object for which you want to set access controls and select **Properties** from the pop-up menu or the **File** menu. In the Properties window, select the Authorization tab. See "Specifying Access Controls" on page 115 for information about setting access controls from the Authorization tab.

CAUTION:
Use extreme caution when making any changes to these resources. Changing the permissions on a resource could make the resource unavailable to applications and users. △

6 After you have set the access controls, click [OK] to close the Properties window.

Controlling Access to Resources

After you have located the metadata objects that represent the resources for which you want to control access, you can use the controls provided by the Authorization Manager to implement the access controls. Access controls for a metadata object are specified using any of these methods:

☐ specifying the access controls directly on the Authorization tab of the object's Properties window

☐ applying an access control template (ACT), which is a named set of access controls that can be applied to multiple objects

☐ using access controls that are inherited from parent objects or that are set through the repository ACT, which specifies the default access controls for all objects in a repository.

Understanding the Authorization Tab

The Authorization tab in the Properties window for a metadata object specifies the access controls that are in place for the object. The controls can be set directly from the tab, inherited, or set through an ACT. A typical Authorization tab for an object follows:

Display 7.7   Authorization Tab

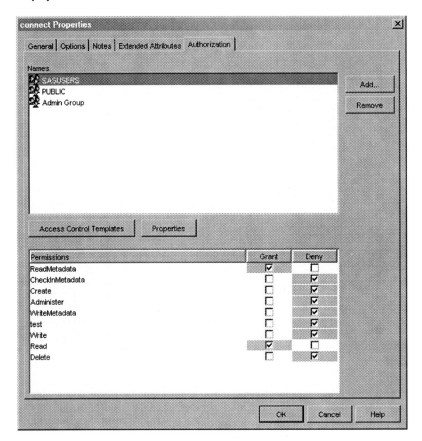

The **Names** list contains the users and groups for who access controls have been specified for the object. In the preceding display, the groups SASUSERS, PUBLIC, and Admin Group have access controls listed on the tab that specify how each group can use the object.

The **Permissions** list contains the permissions that are specified for the user or group that is currently selected in the **Names** list. The **Permissions** list displays each type of permission and specifies whether the permission is granted or denied for the selected user or group. In the preceding display, the SASUSERS group is granted ReadMetadata and Read permissions, and denied all other permissions.

The color of the background on each permission indicates whether the permission has been directly specified for the object, inherited from a parent object, or inherited from the repository ACT. The background colors and their meanings are as follows:

Gray background color	specifies that the permission was either set in the repository ACT or in a parent object.
Green background color	specifies that the permission was set by an ACT that has been associated with the metadata object.

No background color specifies that the permission was set by an access control specified for the object and the selected user or group.

Specifying Access Controls

To apply access controls to an object for a user or group:

1 Select a metadata definition in the navigation tree or the display area and select **Properties** from the pop-up menu or **File** menu. In the Properties window, select the Authorization tab.

Display 7.8 Blank Authorization Tab

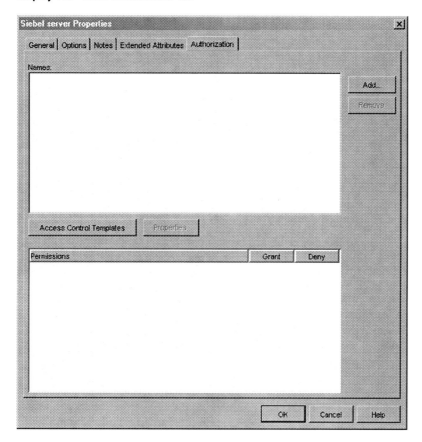

In this example, no permissions are defined for the object. However, in most cases, the Authorization tab displays the controls defined in the repository ACT.

2 To create an access control for a user or group, click Add to display the Add Users and/or Groups window.

Display 7.9   Add Users and/or Groups Window

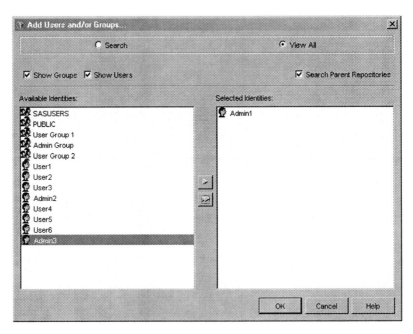

3 Select the user or group for whom you want to specify an access control from the **Available Identities** list, then use the arrow controls to move that user or group to the **Selected Identities** list. Click ⌷OK⌷ to return to the Authorization tab.

Display 7.10   Add Users and/or Groups Window – User Selected

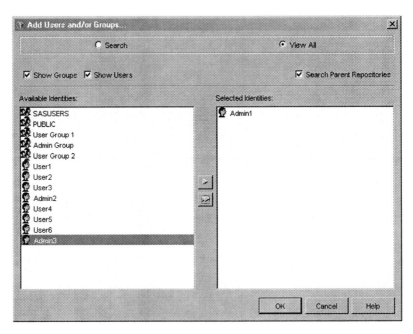

4 The Authorization tab now displays the default permission settings for the selected user or group. The settings from the repository ACT (if one has been designated) are displayed.

Display 7.11   Authorization Tab – Default Permission Settings for a User

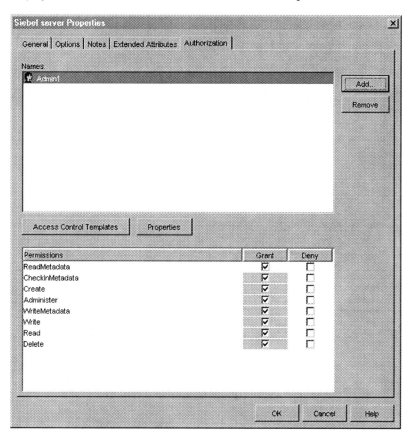

5 To change the value for a permission, click the value (**Grant** or **Deny**) that you want to set. Values you set while creating the access control take precedence over other permissions that apply to the user or group, whether inherited or set through an ACT.

Display 7.12 Authorization Tab – User Permissions Set

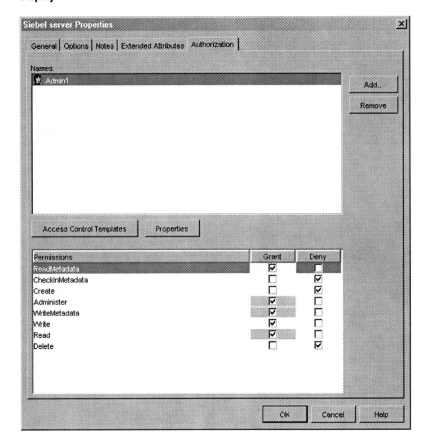

6 When you have finished specifying access controls for the metadata object, click [OK] to close the Properties window and apply the authorization settings.

Working with Access Control Templates

If you have access controls that you want to apply to users or groups for many different metadata objects, you can create an access control template (ACT). An ACT is a named set of authorization settings for a specified set of users that you can re–use for multiple resources. ACTs let you save often-used authorization settings for users and user groups, then apply the settings to a metadata resource by specifying the ACT.

Creating an Access Control Template

To create an access control template:

1 From the navigation tree, select the Authorization Manager plug-in and select the Access Control Templates folder. Select **New Access Control Template** from the pop-up menu, the toolbar, or the **Actions** menu. The New Access Control Template Properties window appears.

Display 7.13 New Access Control Template Properties Window

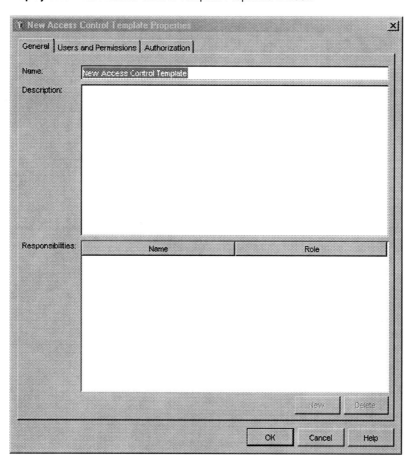

2 Specify the name of the ACT in the **Name** field and (optionally) a description. The **Responsibilities** list allows you to specify descriptive information about users that have specific roles for the template (such as administrator). Select the Users and Permissions tab.

Display 7.14 New Access Control Template Properties Window – Users and Permissions Tab

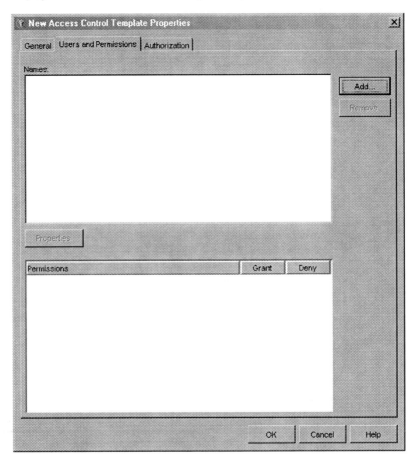

3 The Users and Permissions tab displays the users and groups to which this ACT applies and the permissions that are in effect for each user or group. The list of users and list of permissions are both initially empty when you are creating a new ACT. To add a user or group to the list, click Add to display the Add Users and/or Groups window.

Display 7.15 Add Users and/or Groups Window

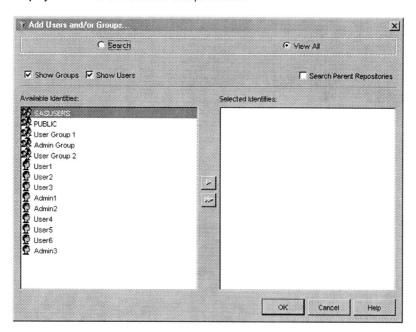

4 Select all of the users and groups to which the ACT should apply in the **Available Identities** list and use the arrow controls to move them to the **Selected Identities** list. The users and groups you select will all have a set of permissions specified in the ACT, but they are not required to have the same set of permissions.

  Select the **View All** and **Search Parent Repositories** check box (selected by default) to find users and groups in all parent repositories for the current repositories. All users and groups should be defined in the foundation repository. You can use the **Show Groups** and **Show Users** check boxes to limit the displayed entries, or you can select the **Search** radio button to find a particular user or group. When you have selected all the identities to which the ACT should apply, click OK to return to the Users and Permissions tab.

5 Select an identity in the **Names** list.

Display 7.16 Users and Permissions Window – User Selected

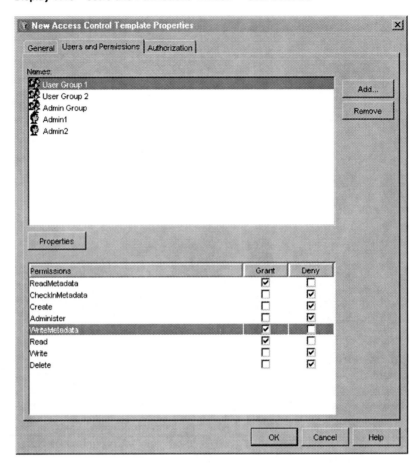

The **Permissions** list specifies the permissions for the selected identity in the ACT. Select the **Grant** or **Deny** check box for the permissions to specify whether the user should be allowed or denied the ability to perform the selected action.

Set the permissions for each user or group in the **Names** list. When you are finished, select the Authorization tab.

6 The Authorization tab specifies the permissions that users and groups have for the current ACT. Permissions listed on the Authorization tab apply to the ACT, not to any other resource. See "Specifying Access Controls" on page 115 for information about specifying permissions from the Authorization tab.

7 Click ⬚OK⬚ to define the access control template.

Applying an ACT to a Metadata Object

After you create one or more ACTs, you can apply them to metadata objects in the repository. If you designate a template as a repository ACT, those controls will be automatically applied to all objects in the repository. Other ACTs are only applied to objects that you choose.

To apply an access control template to a metadata object:

1 Locate the object to which you want to apply the ACT (see "Locating Resources" on page 107 for more information). Select the object, then select **Properties** from the pop-up menu or the **File** menu. In the Properties window, select the Authorization tab.

2 The Authorization tab lists any access controls that have already been specified for the object, whether directly or through the repository ACT.

Display 7.17 Authorization Tab For a Defined Object

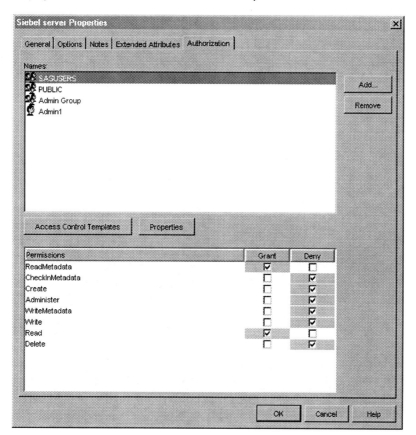

3 Click Access Control Templates to display the Add/Remove Access Control Templates window.

Display 7.18   Add/Remove Access Control Templates Window

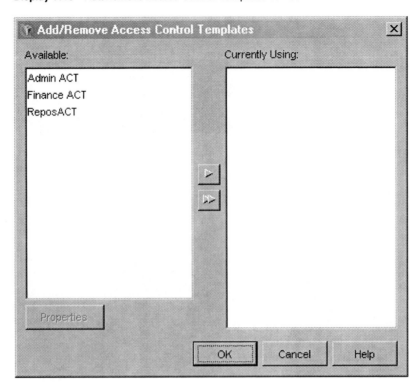

4   The window lists all of the ACTs that have been defined (in the **Available** list) and the templates that have been applied to the object (in the **Currently Using** list).

   Note that the **Currently Using** list only contains ACTs that have been specifically assigned to this object. Although the object uses the settings from the repository ACT (ReposACT in this example), it is not listed in the **Currently Using** list because it was not directly applied to the current object.

   Select a template and click Properties to view information about the access controls specified in the ACT.

5   Select the ACT you want to use in the **Available** list and use the arrow controls to move the template to the **Currently Using** list. You can select more than one template.

Display 7.19 Add/Remove Access Control Templates Window − Template Selected

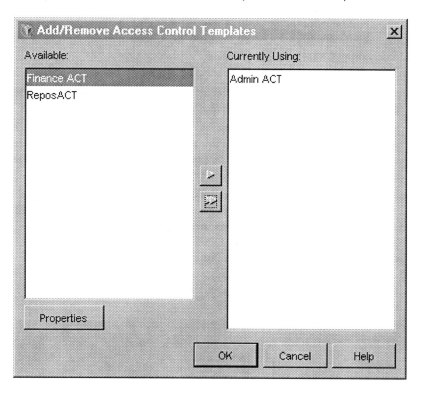

6 Click OK to apply the ACTs to the object.

Controlling Access to a Repository

Modifying the Repository ACT

When you create a metadata repository, a repository ACT is automatically created that specifies default access controls for all objects in the repository. You can modify the permission settings on the repository ACT to provide default settings that meet your security needs.

To modify the repository ACT:

1 From the navigation tree, select the Authorization Manager plug-in, then select the Access Control Templates folder.

2 The folder contains all ACTs that have been defined. The repository ACT is identified by the repository ACT icon ( ).

3 Select the ACT, then select **Properties** from the pop-up menu or the **File** menu.

4 Use the Properties window to make changes to the repository ACT. Remember that the permission settings you choose for the repository ACT will be applied by default to all resources in the repository.

5 Click OK to close the Properties window and apply the changes.

Designating a Different Repository ACT

Rather than modifying the repository ACT, you can designate a different ACT to serve as the repository ACT.

To designate a repository ACT:

1 Select the Authorization Manager plug-in in the navigation tree, and then select the Access Control Templates folder.

2 In the display area, select the ACT that you want to apply to the repository and select **Repository ACT** from the pop-up menu or the **Actions** menu. You can also open the Access Control Templates folder in the navigation tree and select the ACT in the navigation tree.

3 After you designate the repository ACT, the icon for the ACT changes to a blue color. When you display the pop-up menu or **Actions** menu with the repository ACT selected, the **Repository ACT** menu item is selected.

Display 7.20 Repository ACT Menu Designation

Managing Permissions

Although you cannot change any of the default permissions, you can create and manage your own user–defined permissions. After they have been created, user–defined permissions function identically to default permissions and can be set through ACTs and ACEs. User-defined permissions are only used if you are using an application that requires the permission value to enforce authorization decisions. You must be an administrative user or an unrestricted user to manage permissions.

Creating a User-Defined Permission

To create a user-defined permission:

1 From the navigation tree, select the Permissions folder under the Authorization Manager plug-in.

2 Select **New Permission** from the pop-up menu, the **Actions** menu, or the toolbar.

Display 7.21 New Permission Window

3 In the New Permission window, enter a name and (optionally) a description for the permission. Because a user-defined permission only works with applications that have been specifically created to use the permission, you must make sure to specify the permission exactly as the using application expects.

4 Click OK to define the permission. The permission will now be listed with the default permissions when defining ACTs and ACEs.

Modifying a Permission

You can only modify a permission if you are an unrestricted user or if you have been directly granted WriteMetadata permission for the permission object. You can only modify user-defined permissions, not default permissions.

CAUTION:
Each permission can be used by thousands of access controls. Modifying or deleting a permission is likely to have serious consequences for authorization. △

To modify a permission:

1 From the navigation tree, select the Authorization Manager plug-in and then select the Permissions folder.

2 The navigation tree and display area list the defined permissions, including any user-created permissions.

Display 7.22 Permissions Navigation Tree

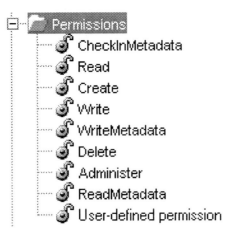

3 To modify a permission, select the permission and select **Properties** from the pop-up menu or the **File** menu.

Display 7.23 Permission Properties Window

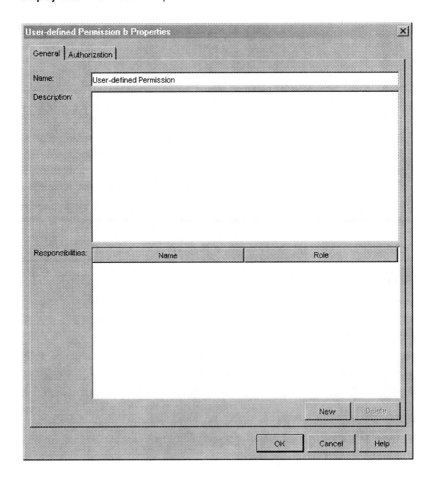

4 You can use the General tab to change the name, description, or responsibility list for the permission. You can also use the Authorization tab to specify the access controls for the permission. Click ⟨OK⟩ to apply the changes.

CHAPTER

8

Managing SAS Licenses

What Is the License Manager?

The License Manager is a SAS Management Console plug-in that provides functions for you to view information about SAS software installed on computers in your organization. When SAS software is installed on these computers, they store metadata about the installation on a SAS Metadata Server, and the License Manager can access and display that metadata.

Using the License Manager, you can

- view information about all SAS installations on a machine (including the version, expiration date, and the name of the installer)

- view information about the SAS components that are included in a selected SAS installation

- view a history of installation activity for a selected machine.

Setting Up the License Manager

In order for the License Manager to be able to access installation information, you must set up an installation metadata server, which is used to store the installation metadata. You can then use SAS Management Console to connect to the server and the License Manager to read the metadata

For Windows installations, you can set up the installation metadata server in two ways:

- Using the SAS Configuration Wizard. This wizard, which is run from the SAS Software Navigator, automatically sets up the install metadata server.

- Using the SAS Configuration Wizard. This wizard prompts you for the following information:

  - server

  - port

  - protocol

  - repository

□ user ID

□ password.

The wizard uses this information to create the metasys.xml file. Each time a SAS installation is performed, the installation process uses the metasys.xml file to determine the location of the installation metadata server.

For UNIX and VMS installations, the SAS Configuration Wizard provides an option of integrating installation information with a SAS metadata server (installation metadata is not stored by default). After you specify that the installation should be integrated, you must provide the following information:

□ server

□ port

□ repository

□ user ID

□ password.

As with Windows installations, this information is saved to a file which the installation process uses to determine the location of the installation metadata server.

Viewing Machine Information

The License Manager lets you view information about the individual machines on which SAS has been installed as well as providing an installation history.

To view machine information:

1 Connect to the installation metadata server. See "Setting Up the License Manager" on page 131 for more information.

2 From the navigation tree, select the Maintenance folder and then the License Manager plug-in to view a list of machines.

3 Select a machine and select **Properties** from the pop-up menu or the **File** menu. The Machine Properties window appears, with the General tab selected.

Display 8.1   Machine Properties Window – General Tab

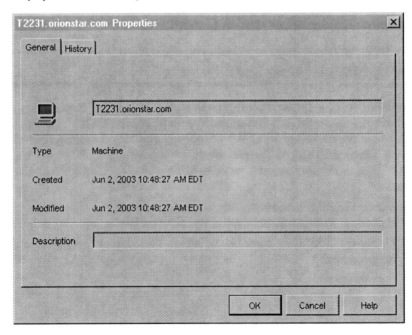

The General tab displays the machine name and lists when the installation information was created and modified. The **Created** field specifies the first time SAS was installed on the machine. The **Modified** field specifies the date and time of the most recent SAS installation.

4 Select the History tab to view details about the installation activity for the machine.

Display 8.2 Machine Properties Window – History Tab

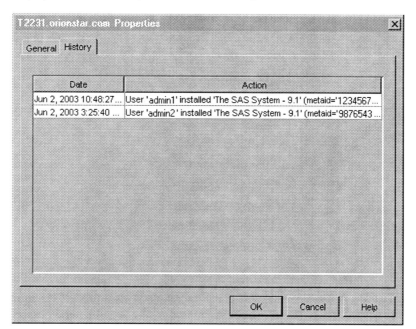

5 Click OK to close the window.

Viewing License Information

To view information about SAS licenses on machines in your organization:

1 Connect to the installation metadata server. See "Setting Up the License Manager" on page 131 for more information.

2 From the navigation tree, select the Maintenance folder and then the License Manager plug-in. The navigation tree lists the machines that have written installation information to the metadata server.

Display 8.3   License Manager Navigation Tree

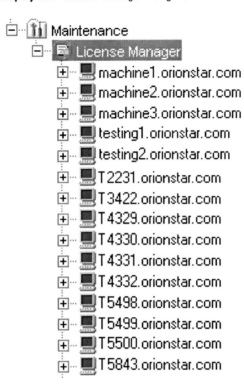

3 To view information about the SAS licenses on a particular machine, either select the machine in the navigation tree or click the plus sign beside the machine.

4 If you select the machine in the navigation tree, the display area contains information about the SAS licenses installed on the machine.

Display 8.4   License Information For Selected Machine

Name	Installed By	Version	Expiration	Date
The SAS System ...	osadmin1	9.01.01B0P05282003	Sep 1, 2003	Jun 2, 2003 3:11:31 P...

If you click the plus sign next to the machine in the navigation tree, the licenses for that machine appear below the machine in the tree.

Display 8.5 License Manager Navigation Tree – Machine Details

5 You can select the license (either in the navigation tree or the display area) and then select **Properties** from the pop-up menu or the **File** menu to open the Properties window for the license.

Display 8.6 License Properties Window

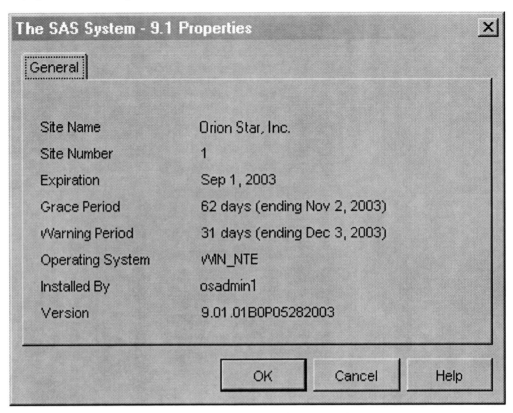

The window displays information about the installation and the expiration of the selected license. Click OK to close the window.

Viewing Component Information

You can choose to view information about the individual SAS components that are licensed and installed on a specified machine.

To view component information:

1 Connect to the installation metadata server. See "Setting Up the License Manager" on page 131 for more information.

2 From the navigation tree, select the Maintenance folder and then select the License Manager plug-in.

3 Select **Options** from the pop-up menu or the **Actions** menu. The Options window appears.

Display 8.7 License Manager Options Window

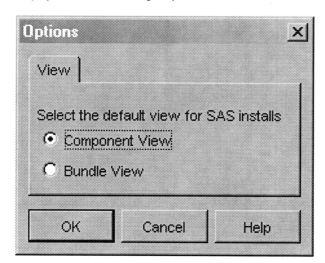

4 In the Options window, select **Component View** and click OK.

5 In the navigation tree, click the plus sign next to a machine name to display the list of SAS installations for the machine. Select a SAS installation in the navigation tree whose components you want to view.

6 The display area lists all of the SAS components that are licensed for the selected machine, their location (if they are currently installed), and the installation date.

Display 8.8 Licensed SAS Components

Product Name	Installation Location	Expiration Date	Language	CPU
Base SAS	C:\Program Files\SAS\SAS 9.1	Sep 1, 2003		
Enterprise Miner	C:\Program Files\SAS\SAS 9.1	Sep 1, 2003		
SAS Integration ...	C:\Program Files\SAS\SAS 9.1	Sep 1, 2003		
SAS/CONNECT	C:\Program Files\SAS\SAS 9.1	Sep 1, 2003		
SAS/EIS	C:\Program Files\SAS\SAS 9.1	Sep 1, 2003		
SAS/ETS	C:\Program Files\SAS\SAS 9.1	Sep 1, 2003		
SAS/FSP	C:\Program Files\SAS\SAS 9.1	Sep 1, 2003		
SAS/GRAPH	C:\Program Files\SAS\SAS 9.1	Sep 1, 2003		
SAS/INSIGHT	C:\Program Files\SAS\SAS 9.1	Sep 1, 2003		
SAS/OR	C:\Program Files\SAS\SAS 9.1	Sep 1, 2003		
SAS Text Miner	C:\Program Files\SAS\SAS 9.1	Sep 1, 2003		

CHAPTER
9

Managing Job Schedules

What Is the Schedule Manager?

The Schedule Manager is a SAS Management Console plug-in that schedules jobs created in other applications (such as SAS Data Integration Studio) or SAS data step or procedure programs stored on a processing server. The jobs can be scheduled either by using Platform Computing's Load Sharing Facility (LSF) or by using the scheduling capabilities of a server's operating system. Using the Schedule Manager, you can

- create job flows, which contain one or more jobs for scheduling.

- create dependencies for jobs in the flow, which are criteria that must be met in order for the job to run. Dependencies can be based on time, other jobs, or files.

- schedule a flow to run based on specified conditions (run once, run manually, or run whenever a dependency is met).

The scheduled flows are run either on a defined scheduling server under the control of the Flow Manager (part of the LSF software) or on a operating system scheduling server.

Setting Up Job Scheduling

Before you can use the Schedule Manager to schedule jobs and job flows, you must complete several tasks to set up the job scheduling environment and prepare jobs for scheduling.

To set up job scheduling using LSF scheduling:

1 In SAS Management Console, create a definition for a SAS server (which includes a workspace server and a batch server) on which scheduled jobs must be run.

2 Install Platform Computing's Load Sharing Facility (LSF) and Process Manager servers.

3 Install Platform Computing's Flow Manager and Calendar Editor.

4 In SAS Management Console, create a metadata definition for an LSF scheduling server.

5 Deploy jobs for scheduling.

To set up job scheduling using operating system scheduling:

1 Create a definition for a SAS server on which scheduled jobs must be run.

2 In SAS Management Console, create a definition for an operating system scheduling server.

3 Deploy jobs for scheduling.

See *SAS Intelligence Platform: System Administration Guide* for details about each of these setup tasks.

Creating Scheduling Server Definitions

Job flows that are scheduled in the Schedule Manager are sent to a server that controls the scheduling and runs the application. You must use the SAS Management Console Server Manager plug-in to create definitions for the servers required to perform scheduling.

To create the scheduling server definitions:

1 Use the Server Manager plug-in to define a SAS workspace server. See "Defining a Basic SAS Server" on page 61 for details about creating a new SAS server definition.

From the navigation tree, select the **Server Manager** plug-in and select **New Server** from the pop-up menu, the **Actions** menu, or the toolbar to start the New Server Wizard.

In the Server Type window in the wizard, select **SAS Application Server** as the server type.

Display 9.1 Server Type Window

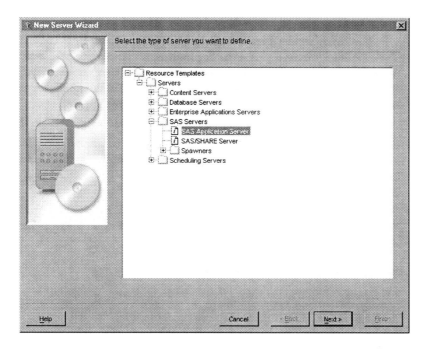

In the SAS Server Type window, select **Workspace Server** as the SAS server type.

Display 9.2 SAS Server Type Window – Workspace Server Selected

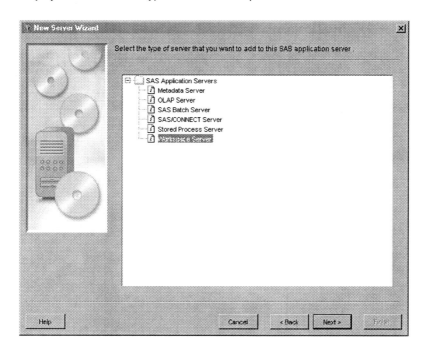

Complete the New Server Wizard to define the SAS workspace server.

2 Use the Server Manager to add an application server component to the server you just defined. See "Adding a SAS Server Component" on page 66 for details.

In the navigation tree, select the SAS application server you just defined, then select **Add Application Server Component** from the pop-up menu, the toolbar, or the **Actions** menu. The New Server Wizard starts.

In the SAS Server Type window, select one of the SAS batch servers as the type of component you want to add. depending on the type of jobs you want to schedule. You can select **SAS Data Step Batch Server** (for scheduling SAS DATA step programs), **SAS Java Batch Server** (for scheduling java programs), or **SAS Generic Batch Server** (for all other scheduling applications.

Complete the wizard to add the SAS batch server to the application server.

After you have defined the workspace server and batch server, you must specify a directory that will store the code for the jobs deployed for scheduling. This directory must be available to the SAS workspace server.

To define the scheduling directory:

1 From the navigation tree, select the Schedule Manager plug-in, then select **Deployment Directories** from the **Actions** menu or the pop–up menu. The Deployment Directories window appears.

Display 9.3   Deployment Directories Window

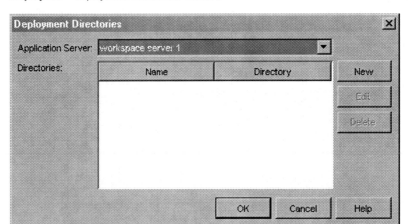

2 Select the workspace server that will be used for scheduling from the **Application Server** drop-down list.

3 Click **New** to display the New Directory window. Specify the name and path for the deployment directory.

Display 9.4   New Directory Window

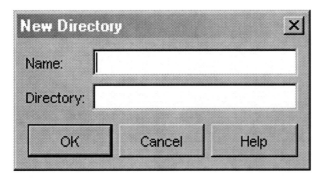

4 Click **OK** to close the New Directory window, then click **OK** to close the Deployment Directories window.

Installing Load Sharing Facility and Process Manager Servers

After you have created definitions for the workspace server and batch server, you must install Platform Computing's Load Sharing Facility and the Process Manager server. See *SAS Intelligence Platform: System Administration Guide* for installation information.

Installing Flow Manager and Calendar Editor

You must install the Flow Manager and the Calendar Editor on the machine where SAS Management Console is installed. The Flow Manager is a Platform Computing scheduling client that manages the status of flows that are submitted to an LSF server. The Calendar Editor is a Platform Computing scheduling client that enables you to create custom calendars that are used to create time dependencies for jobs.

See *SAS Intelligence Platform: System Administration Guide* for installation information.

Specifying Metadata for an LSF Scheduling Server

After installing and starting the Process Manager server, you must create a metadata definition in SAS Management Console to identify the server.

To create the Process Manager server definition:

1 From the navigation tree, select the **Server Manager** plug-in, then select **New Server** from the pop-up menu, the **Actions** menu, or the toolbar. The New Server Wizard starts.

2 In the Server Type window, select **Platform Process Manager Server** as the server type you want to define.

3 Follow the windows in the New Server Wizard to define the server. In the Connection Options window, specify the authentication domain, host and port number for the Process Manager server you previously installed and started (see "Installing Load Sharing Facility and Process Manager Servers" on page 143).

Display 9.5   Connection Options Window for Process Manager Server

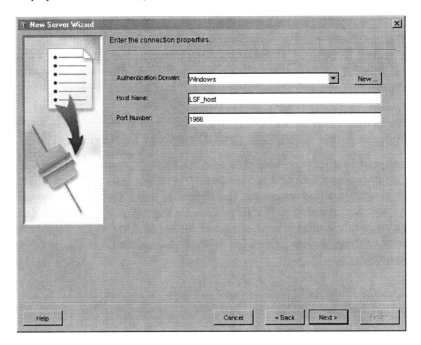

4 Complete the New Server Wizard to create a definition for the Process Manager server.

Defining an Operating System Scheduling Server

If you are going to use operating system scheduling capabilities to schedule jobs, you must define one or more servers that will be used to run the scheduled jobs. To define an operating system scheduling server, follow these steps:

1 From the navigation tree, select the **Server Manager** plug-in, then select **New Server** from the pop-up menu, the **Actions** menu, or the toolbar. The New Server Wizard starts.

2 In the Server Type page of the wizard, select **Operating System Services** as the server type.

3 Follow the prompts in the wizard to define the server.

Deploying Jobs for Scheduling

After you have installed the required software and started and defined the necessary servers, you can begin preparing jobs to be scheduled. The Schedule Manager only schedules jobs from other applications that have been deployed (prepared for scheduling).

To deploy a job for scheduling in an application such as SAS Data Integration Studio:

1 Select the job to be scheduled.

2 Select the appropriate option in the application to display the Deploy for Scheduling window.

3 Specify the scheduling server as the server to which the job should be deployed, then specify the other information requested by the window.

4 The scheduling server generates SAS code for the job, and metadata for the deployed job is stored in the current metadata repository. The job is now available to be scheduled using the Schedule Manager.

For detailed information about deploying jobs from a specific application, see the online Help for the application.

Deploying DATA Step Programs for Scheduling

You can also deploy for scheduling DATA step or procedure programs that are stored on a SAS DATA step batch server. Once you have deployed a DATA step program, you can add the program to a flow and define dependencies just as you would for jobs deployed by other SAS applications.

To deploy a DATA step or procedure program for scheduling:

1 If you have not already done so, use the Server Manager to define a SAS DATA step batch server. The program you want to deploy must be stored on the DATA step batch server machine.

2 From the navigation tree, select the **Schedule Manager** plug-in, then select **Deploy SAS Data Step Program** from the pop-up menu.

3 In the Deploy SAS Data Step Program dialog box, select the SAS DATA step batch server that contains the program you want to deploy.

4 In the **Deployment Directory** field, select or define the directory that contains the program to be deployed.

5 Select the DATA step program in the **File** field and the name you want to use for the job in the **Deployed Job Name** field.

6 When you click **OK**, the metadata for the deployed job is stored in the metadata repository. The job is now available to be scheduled using the Schedule Manager.

Creating a Job Flow

In order to schedule a job, you must first add it to a job flow or create a new job flow. A job flow is a group of jobs and their dependencies.

To create a job flow:

1 From the navigation tree, select the Schedule Manager plug-in, then select **New Flow** from the **Actions** menu, the pop-up menu, or the toolbar. The New Job Flow window appears.

Display 9.6   New Job Flow Window

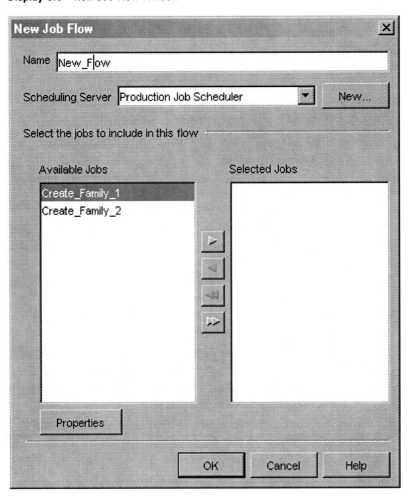

2   In the New Job Flow window, provide a name for the job flow, then select the scheduling server and the jobs that the flow should contain. The drop-down list for the **Scheduling Server** field lists all of the defined Process Manager and operating system scheduling servers (see "Specifying Metadata for an LSF Scheduling Server" on page 143). Select the server that you want to use to run the current job flow.

   The **Available Jobs** field lists all of the jobs that have been defined and deployed for scheduling (see "Deploying Jobs for Scheduling" on page 144). Select a job and use the arrow controls to move the job to the **Selected Jobs** list to include it in the job flow.

3   Click OK to close the window and create the job flow.

Specifying Dependencies

After you have created a job flow, you can specify dependencies for the job flow. Without dependencies, all of the jobs in the job flow run immediately and simultaneously. Dependencies let you specify the conditions that must be met before a job in a job flow runs.

To create a dependency for a job flow:

1 From the navigation tree, select the Schedule Manager plug-in and select the job flow whose dependencies you want to create. Click the plus sign next to the job flow to display the jobs that are contained in the job flow. Select a job for which you want to specify dependencies and select `Dependencies` from the pop–up menu, the `Actions` menu, or the toolbar. The Dependencies window appears.

Display 9.7 Dependencies Window

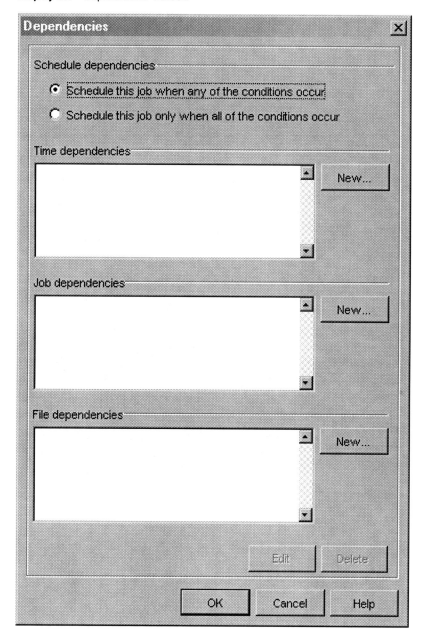

2 The Dependencies window lets you specify time dependencies (the job runs at a specified time or day), job dependencies (the job runs based on another job), and file dependencies (the job runs based on conditions associated with a specified file). You can also specify whether the job runs only when certain dependencies are met, or if all dependencies must be met.

3 Click New next to the `Time dependencies` list to define a new time dependency. A time dependency specifies that the job runs on a specified day at a specified time.

Display 9.8 New Time Dependency Window – Process Manager Scheduling

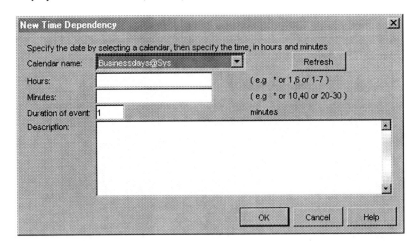

If you are defining a job to run on a Process Manager server, you must first select the calendar from the **Calendar name** drop-down list. The calendar identifies the days for the dependency. Several sample calendars are supplied with the LSF Scheduler software, and you can also create your own calendars. Refer to the online Help for the Schedule Manager plug–in for more information.

For a job running on a Process Manager server, after you specify the calendar, use the **Hours** and **Minutes** fields to specify the time at which the job runs. Specify how long the job should run in the **Duration of event** field. Click OK when you have finished defining the dependency.

If you are defining a job to run on an operating system scheduling server, you must specify the start date and recurrence pattern for the dependency. Some recurrence patterns are not supported on all operating systems. Refer to the online Help for the Schedule Manager for specific restrictions for your operating system.

4 Click New next to the **Job dependencies** list to define a job dependency. A job dependency specifies that the current job runs if a specified event occurs with another job. For example, you can specify that the current job runs when Job A completes successfully, or you can specify that it runs when Job A ends with a specified exit code.

Display 9.9 New Job Dependency Window

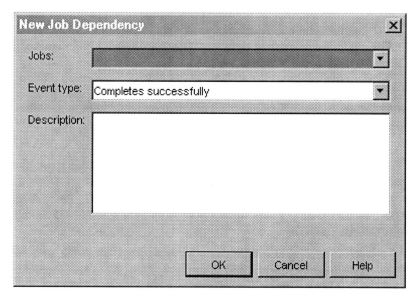

In the New Job Dependency window, select the job that the current job is dependent on from the **Jobs** drop-down list, then select the event that is part of the dependency from the **Event Type** drop-down list (such as successful completion, ending with a specified exit code, or failing to start). Some event types require you to specify additional information (such as an exit code or a run time) that is part of the dependency. Click OK when you have finished defining the dependency.

5 Click New next to the **File dependencies** list to define a file dependency. A file dependency specifies that the current job runs if a condition is met on a specified file. For example, you can specify that the current job runs whenever File B is created, or that it runs when File B becomes larger than a specified size.

Display 9.10 New File Dependency Window

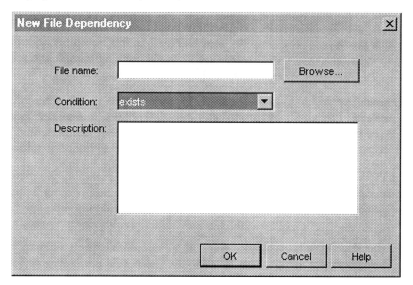

In the New File Dependency window, specify the file upon which the job is dependent in the **File name** field and the file state that must exist in the

`Condition` field (such as that the file exists, that the file is a specified size, or that the file is beyond a certain age). Click $\boxed{\text{OK}}$ when you have finished defining the dependency.

6 When you have finished defining dependencies for the selected job, click $\boxed{\text{OK}}$ in the Dependencies window.

Scheduling Flows

After you have created a job flow and (optionally) defined dependencies for the jobs in the job flow, you can schedule the flow to run. Scheduled job flows are sent to the scheduling server, where the dependencies are evaluated. You can specify that a selected job flow is scheduled to run according to a specified trigger.

To schedule a job flow:

1 From the navigation tree, select the `Schedule Manager` and select the job flow you want to schedule. Select `Schedule Flow` from the pop-up menu, the toolbar, or the `Actions` menu. The Schedule Flow window appears.

Display 9.11 Schedule Flow Window

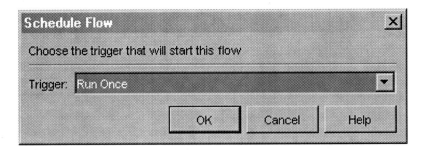

2 Select the condition under which the flow should run from the `Trigger` drop-down list. Valid values are

`Run Once`	specifies that the flow is sent to the scheduling server, which evaluates any dependencies and runs the jobs in the job flow one time only.
`Manually in Scheduling Server`	specifies that the flow is sent to the scheduling server, which evaluates any dependencies but does not run the jobs in the job flow. The job flow is held until someone uses the Flow Manager application (part of the LSF Scheduler software) to manually run the jobs.
\<selected dependency\>	specifies that a defined dependency is a trigger for the job flow. A job flow that uses a dependency as a trigger runs each time the conditions for the dependency are met.

3 After you have scheduled a flow on a Process Manager server, you can use the Flow Manager application to view the history of a job flow or job, rerun a job flow or job, or stop a job flow from running. If you scheduled the flow on an operating system scheduling server, you can use operating system commands to view the status of a flow or manually stop the flow from running. See the Help for the Schedule Manager plug-in or the Flow Manager application for information.

Viewing Job Flow Properties

After you have created and scheduled a job flow, you can use the Schedule Manager to view properties for the job flow or jobs that are part of the job flow. Select a job flow or job in the navigation tree and then select **Properties** from the pop-up menu or the **File** menu. You can also use the Properties window to define authorization settings for the job flow or job. See "Controlling Access to Resources" on page 113 for more information.

Adding Jobs to a Job Flow

You can also add jobs to an existing job flow. Select a job flow, then select **Add a Job** from the pop-up menu, the toolbar, or the **Actions** menu. Use the Add Job window to select from the jobs that have been deployed for scheduling.

Display 9.12 Add Job Window

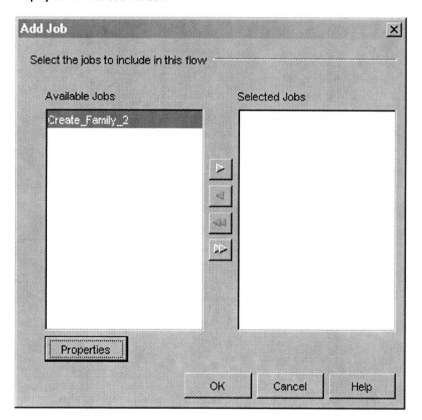

CHAPTER

10

Managing XMLMaps

What Is the XMLMap Manager?

The XMLMap Manager is a SAS Management Console plug-in that allows you to create, import, and manage XMLMaps. An XMLMap is an XML file that tells the SAS XML LIBNAME engine (SXLE) how to interpret XML markup as SAS data sets, columns, and rows.

Using the XMLMap Manager, you can

□ import an existing XMLMap

□ create a new XMLMap

□ manage XMLMaps (including renaming and deleting).

Importing an XMLMap

If you have an existing XMLMap, can use the XMLMap Manager to import the file into the metadata server.

To import an XMLMap:

1 From the navigation tree, select the XMLMap Manager, then select **Import XMLMap** from the pop-up menu or the **Actions** menu.

2 In the Open window, select the XMLMap you want to import and click [Open].

Display 10.1 Open Window

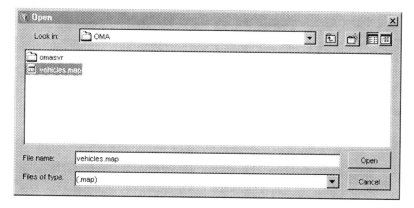

3 The imported XMLMap is listed in the navigation tree underneath the XMLMap Manager plug-in.

Display 10.2 XMLMap Manager Navigation Tree

The name of the imported XMLMap is set to the value of the name= attribute on the SXLE element tag. The name must be unique within the metadata repository, and cannot be SXLEMAP or XMLMAP.

4 Selecting a table name contained in the XMLMap from the navigation tree displays the column names and attributes in the display area.

Display 10.3 XMLMap Column Names and Attributes

Column Name	Description	Length	Type	Datatype	Format	Informat
Year			Numeric	integer		
Model		8	Character	string		

Creating an XMLMap

To create an XMLMap:

1 From the navigation tree, select the XMLMap Manager plug-in, then select **Create XMLMap** from the pop-up menu or the **Actions** menu. The XML Mapper application starts.

Display 10.4 XML Mapper Application Window

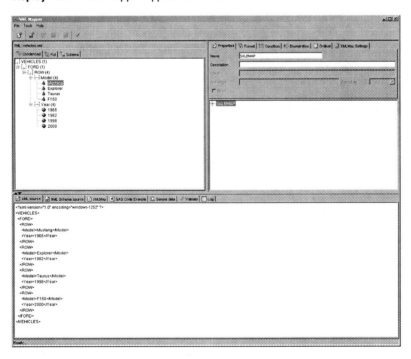

2 Create an XMLMap file in the XML Mapper application by opening the XML file whose data you want to map, and then using the XML attributes to define the required mapping. For information about using the XML Mapper application, refer to the application's Help.

3 When you save the new XMLMap and close the XML Mapper application, the new XMLMap is listed under the XMLMap Manager plug-in.

Managing XMLMaps

You can use the XMLMap Manager to rename or delete an XMLMap.

To rename an XMLMap, select the XMLMap in the navigation tree or the display area and select **Rename XMLMap** from the pop-up menu or the **Actions** menu.

Display 10.5 Rename XMLMap Window

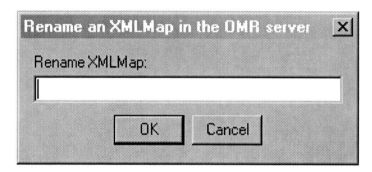

Specify a new name for the XMLMap in the Rename window and click [OK]. Each XMLMap name must be unique within the metadata repository, and you cannot use the names SXLEMAP or XMLMAP.

To delete an XMLMap, select the XMLMap in the navigation tree or the display area and select **Delete XMLMap** from the pop-up menu or the **Actions** menu. The application asks you to confirm the deletion.

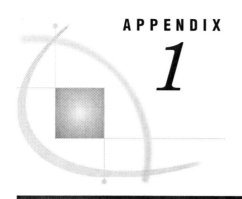

1

Replication and Promotion Macros

Modifying Replication and Promotion Macros **157**

Modifying Replication and Promotion Macros

During the process of running a replication or promotion job, a series of user-defined macros are called. These macros allow you to define additional processing that should take place as part of the replication or promotion job.

The following table lists the macros that you can define or modify.

Table A1.1   Replication and Promotion User Macros

Macro name	Function
mduval.sas	Stores any user-defined validation code.
mdpresrc.sas	Stores user-defined code to run before the source repository is copied to the work directory on the source server.
mdpstsrc.sas	Stores user-defined code to run after the source repository has been copied to the work directory on the source server.
mdcptrg.sas	Specifies the method by which data sets are copied (the default is PROC UPLOAD). Change this value to use a different method.
mdpretg.sas	Stores user-defined code to run before the repository is copied from the work directory to the target repository.
mdpsttrg.sas	Stores user-defined code to run after the repository is copied from the work directory to the target repository.

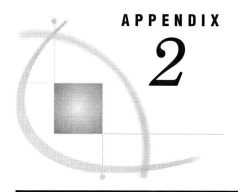

APPENDIX

2

Recommended Reading

Recommended Reading

Here is the recommended reading list for this title:

- □ *Getting Started with the SAS Open Metadata Interface*
- □ *SAS Data Integration Studio: User's Guide*
- □ *SAS Intelligence Platform: Application Server Administration Guide*
- □ *SAS Intelligence Platform: Installation Guide*
- □ *SAS Intelligence Platform: Security Administration Guide*
- □ *SAS Intelligence Platform: System Administration Guide*
- □ *SAS Language Reference: Dictionary*
- □ *SAS Open Metadata Interface: Reference*
- □ *SAS Open Metadata Interface: User's Guide*
- □ *SAS XML LIBNAME Engine User's Guide*
- □ *SAS/ACCESS for Relational Databases: Reference*

For a complete list of SAS publications, see the current *SAS Publishing Catalog*. To order the most current publications or to receive a free copy of the catalog, contact a SAS representative at

SAS Publishing Sales
SAS Campus Drive
Cary, NC 27513
Telephone: (800) 727-3228*
Fax: (919) 677-8166
E-mail: **sasbook@sas.com**
Web address: **support.sas.com/pubs**
* For other SAS Institute business, call (919) 677-8000.

Customers outside the United States should contact their local SAS office.

Glossary

access control template

a reusable named authorization pattern that you can apply to multiple resources. An access control template (ACT) consists of a list of users and groups and indicates, for each user or group, whether permissions are granted or denied.

administrative user

a special user of the metadata server who can create and delete user definitions and logins. An administrative user can also perform administrative tasks such as starting, stopping, pausing, and refreshing the metadata server. Unlike an unrestricted user, an administrative user does not have unrestricted access to the metadata. You are an administrative user if your user ID is listed in the adminUsers.txt file or if you connect to the metadata server using the same user ID that was used to start the metadata server.

application server

a server that is used for storing applications. Users can access and use these server applications instead of loading the applications on their client machines. The application that the client runs is stored on the client. Requests are sent to the server for processing, and the results are returned to the client. In this way, little information is processed by the client, and nearly everything is done by the server.

authentication

the process of verifying the identity of a person or process within the guidelines of a specific security policy.

authentication domain

a set of computing resources that use the same authentication process. An individual uses the same user ID and password for all of the resources in a particular authentication domain. Authentication domains provide logical groupings for resources and logins in a metadata repository. For example, when an application needs to locate credentials that enable a particular user to access a particular server, the application searches the metadata for logins that are associated with the authentication domain in which the target server is registered.

authorization

the process of evaluating rules to determine which users have which permissions for which resources. For example, an authorization rule can specify that a particular user has read and write permissions for a specific database table.

change management
in the SAS Open Metadata Architecture, a facility for metadata source control, metadata promotion, and metadata replication. See also metadata source control, metadata promotion, metadata replication, SAS Open Metadata Architecture.

change-managed repository
in the SAS Open Metadata Architecture, a metadata repository that is under metadata source control. See also change management, metadata source control, metadata repository.

custom repository
in the SAS Open Metadata Architecture, a metadata repository with dependencies. A custom repository is often used to specify resources that are unique to a particular data collection. A custom repository often depends on (inherits metadata from) a foundation repository. For example, a custom repository could define sources and targets that are unique to a particular data warehouse in a test environment. The custom repository could inherit most server metadata from a foundation repository in the test environment. See also foundation repository, source, target, metadata repository, SAS Open Metadata Architecture.

database management system (DBMS)
a software application that enables you to create and manipulate data that is stored in the form of databases. See also hierarchical structure, relational database management system.

default access control template
the access control template (ACT) that controls access to a particular repository and to resources for which definitive access controls are not specified. You can designate one default ACT for each metadata repository. The default ACT is also called the repository ACT.

foundation repository
in the SAS Open Metadata Architecture, a metadata repository that does not depend on other repositories. A foundation repository is often used to specify metadata for global resources. For example, a foundation repository could define most of the servers that are used in several data warehouses in a test environment. See also SAS Open Metadata Architecture, metadata repository, global resources.

group
a collection of users who are registered in a SAS metadata environment. A group can contain other groups as well as individual users. In a SAS metadata environment, a user group is represented by an IdentityGroup object.

hierarchical structure
in SYSTEM 2000 software, an arrangement of data in which records occur at distinct levels with different types of information at each level. Records are related to other records as ancestors, descendants, siblings, and so on.

identity
an individual user or a group of users that is registered in a SAS metadata environment. Each individual and group that accesses secured resources on a SAS Metadata Server should be represented by a unique identity within that server.

job
a metadata object that specifies processes that create output.

job flow
a group of jobs and their dependencies - including dependencies on other jobs, on files, or on specified dates and times. See also job.

login

a combination of a user ID, a password, and an authentication domain. Each login provides access to a particular set of computing resources. In a SAS metadata environment, each login can belong to only one individual or group. However, each individual or group can own multiple logins.

metadata

a description or definition of data or information.

metadata profile

a client-side definition of where a metadata server is located. The definition includes a host name, a port number, and a list of one or more metadata repositories. In addition, the metadata profile can contain a user's login information and instructions for connecting to the metadata server automatically.

metadata promotion

in the SAS Open Metadata Architecture, a feature that enables you to copy the contents of a metadata repository to another repository – and to specify changes in the metadata that will be stored in the target repository. For example, you can use this feature to move metadata from a development environment to a testing environment. In such a scenario, you would probably have to change some ports, hosts, and/or schema names as the metadata moved from one environment to another. See also metadata repository, change management, SAS Open Metadata Architecture.

metadata replication

in the SAS Open Metadata Architecture, a feature that enables you to copy the contents of a metadata repository to another repository. Use replication to make an exact copy of a metadata repository in a new location: to back up a repository, for example. See also metadata repository, change management, SAS Open Metadata Architecture.

metadata repository

a collection of related metadata objects, such as the metadata for a set of tables and columns that are maintained by an application. A SAS Metadata Repository is an example.

metadata server

a server that provides metadata management services to one or more client applications. A SAS Metadata Server is an example.

metadata source control

in the SAS Open Metadata Architecture, a feature that enables multiple users to work with the same metadata repository at the same time – without overwriting each other's changes. See also metadata repository, change management, SAS Open Metadata Architecture.

owner

the person who formulates policy for an object such as a table or a library. See also administrator.

permission

the type of access that a user or group has to a resource. The permission defines what the user or group can do with the resource. Examples of permissions are ReadMetadata and WriteMetadata.

permission condition

a constraint on the explicitly granted permissions for a particular resource. You can use a permission condition to grant access to a specific portion, or slice, of data within a resource. For example, if an OLAP cube has an EmployeeInfo dimension that includes a Salary level, you could give a particular user access to data for only those employees who have salaries that are less than $50,000 per year.

plug-in

a file that modifies, enhances, or extends the capabilities of an application program. The application program must be designed to accept plug-ins, and the plug-ins must meet design criteria specified by the developers of the application program. In SAS Management Console, a plug-in is a JAR file that is installed in the SAS Management Console directory to provide a specific administrative function. The plug-ins enable users to customize SAS Management Console to include only the functions that are needed.

project repository

in the SAS Open Metadata Architecture, a metadata repository that enables a specified person to add or update metadata in a change-managed repository. See also SAS Open Metadata Architecture, metadata repository, change-managed repository.

promotion

The process of copying a metadata repository to another location while making changes to values of metadata attributes. See also replication.

relational database management system

a database management system that organizes and accesses data according to relationships between data items. The main characteristic of a relational database management system is the two-dimensional table. Examples of relational database management systems are DB2, Oracle, SYBASE, and Microsoft SQL Server.

replication

The process of copying a metadata repository to another location without making any changes to values of metadata attributes. See also promotion.

repository access control template

the access control template (ACT) that controls access to a particular repository and to resources for which definitive access controls are not specified. You can designate one default ACT for each metadata repository. The repository ACT is also called the default ACT.

repository dependency

in the SAS Open Metadata Architecture, a relationship between metadata repositories in which one repository inherits metadata from another repository. This relationship can be defined in the wizard that is used to add or update metadata repositories, or it can be defined in the Metadata Manager in SAS Management Console. See also SAS Open Metadata Architecture, metadata repository.

resource

any object that is registered in a metadata repository. For example, a resource can be an application, a data store, a dimension in an OLAP cube, a metadata item, an access control template, or a password.

resource template

A XML file that specifies the information required to create a metadata definition for a SAS resource.

SAS application server

a server that provides SAS services to a client. In the SAS Open Metadata Architecture, the metadata for a SAS application server specifies one or more server components that provide SAS services to a client. See also server, server component.

SAS batch server

in general, a SAS application server that is running in batch mode. In the SAS Open Metadata Architecture, the metadata for a SAS batch server specifies the network address of a SAS Workspace Server, and a SAS start command that will run jobs in batch mode on the SAS Workspace Server. See also SAS Open Metadata Architecture, SAS Workspace Server.

SAS Management Console

a Java application that provides a single user interface for performing SAS administrative tasks.

SAS Metadata Server

a multi-user server that enables users to read metadata from or write metadata to one or more SAS Metadata Repositories. The SAS Metadata Server uses the Integrated Object Model (IOM), which is provided with SAS Integration Technologies, to communicate with clients and with other servers.

SAS Open Metadata Architecture

a general-purpose metadata management facility that provides metadata services to SAS applications. The SAS Open Metadata Architecture enables applications to exchange metadata, which makes it easier for these applications to work together.

SAS Workspace Server

a SAS IOM server that is launched in order to fulfill client requests for IOM workspaces. See also IOM server, workspace.

SAS/ACCESS LIBNAME statement

a statement that specifies a SAS/ACCESS engine that enables you to access the corresponding database management system as if it were a SAS library. See also SAS/ACCESS software.

SAS/ACCESS software

a group of software interfaces, each of which makes data from a particular external database management system (DBMS) directly available to SAS, as well as making SAS data directly available to the DBMS.

schema

a map or model of the overall data structure of a database. A schema consists of schema records that are organized in a hierarchical tree structure. Schema records contain schema items.

server

a computer system that provides data or services to multiple users on a network. The term 'server' sometimes refers to the computer system's hardware and software, but it often refers only to the software that provides the data or services. In a network, users might log on to a file server (to store and retrieve data files), a print server (to use centrally located printers), or a database server (to query or update databases). In a client/server implementation, a server is a program that waits for and fulfills requests from client programs for data or services. The client programs might be running on the same computer or on other computers. See also service, Web server, application server, SAS Metadata Server.

server component

in SAS Management Console, a metadata object that specifies connection information to a particular kind of SAS server on a particular machine. See also SAS Management Console, metadata object, server context, logical server.

service

one or more application components that an authorized user or application can call at any time to provide results that conform to a published specification. For example, network services transmit data or provide conversion of data in a network, database services provide for the storage and retrieval of data in a database, and Web services interact with each other on the World Wide Web. See also Web services, SAS Foundation Services.

source

in SAS ETL Studio, a table, a view, or a file from which you will extract information. Sources can be in any format that SAS can access, on any supported hardware platform. The metadata for a source is an input to a job. See also metadata, job.

target

in SAS ETL Studio, a table, a view, or a file that contains information that has been extracted from a source. Targets can be in any format that SAS can access, on any supported hardware platform. A target is an output of a job. See also source, job.

unrestricted user

a special user of the metadata server who can access all metadata on the server (except for passwords, which an unrestricted user can overwrite but cannot read). An unrestricted user can also perform administrative tasks such as starting, stopping, pausing, and refreshing the metadata server. You are an unrestricted user if your user ID is listed in the adminUsers.txt file and is preceded by an asterisk.

user

a person who is registered in a SAS metadata environment.

Web server

a server machine and software that enable organizations to share information through intranets and through the Internet.

Index

Your Turn

If you have comments or suggestions about *SAS 9.1.3® Management Console: User's Guide*, please send them to us on a photocopy of this page, or send us electronic mail.

For comments about this book, please return the photocopy to

SAS Publishing
SAS Campus Drive
Cary, NC 27513
E-mail: **yourturn@sas.com**

For suggestions about the software, please return the photocopy to

SAS Institute Inc.
Technical Support Division
SAS Campus Drive
Cary, NC 27513
E-mail: **suggest@sas.com**

SAS® Publishing gives you the tools to flourish in any environment with SAS®!

Whether you are new to the workforce or an experienced professional, you need to distinguish yourself in this rapidly changing and competitive job market. SAS® Publishing provides you with a wide range of resources—including publications, online training, and software—to help you set yourself apart.

Expand Your Knowledge with Books from SAS® Publishing

SAS® Press offers user-friendly books for all skill levels, covering such topics as univariate and multivariate statistics, linear models, mixed models, fixed effects regression, and more. View our complete catalog and get free access to the latest reference documentation by visiting us online.

support.sas.com/pubs

SAS® Self-Paced e-Learning Puts Training at Your Fingertips

You are in complete control of your learning environment with SAS Self-Paced e-Learning! Gain immediate 24/7 access to SAS training directly from your desktop, using only a standard Web browser. If you do not have SAS installed, you can use SAS® Learning Edition for all Base SAS e-learning.

support.sas.com/selfpaced

Build Your SAS Skills with SAS® Learning Edition

SAS skills are in demand, and hands-on knowledge is vital. SAS users at all levels, from novice to advanced, will appreciate this inexpensive, intuitive, and easy-to-use personal learning version of SAS. With SAS Learning Edition, you have a unique opportunity to gain SAS software experience and propel your career in new and exciting directions.

support.sas.com/LE

§sas. | SAS Publishing

THE POWER TO KNOW®

LaVergne, TN USA
27 July 2010
191007LV00001B/3/A